ENRICHED SOCIAL STUDIES TEACHING

Through the Use of Games and Activities

E. Richard Churchill
Linda R. Churchill

 FEARON PUBLISHERS
Belmont, California

ISBN-0-8224-2705-2

Library of Congress Catalog Card Number: 72-97017
Printed in the United States of America.

To Gerry and Marilyn

CONTENTS

■ INTRODUCTION

"Dead as bones: dry as dust."

In six short words the study and teaching of social studies have been condemned. All too often, this condemnation has been fully justified. In the hands of an interested and creative teacher, the ideas presented in this volume can make the social studies class a more stimulating, enjoyable, and rewarding experience.

History and social studies are taught in grades four through twelve, as a general rule. Students at the junior and senior high school levels can profit most from the use of the enrichment materials presented in this volume. This is not to say that each and every item may be used successfully at every grade level. However, most ideas given here may be used at a variety of levels of instruction with only slight modification as to format or technique.

The games, presentation ideas, puzzles, and activities described here have been used in classrooms. They do work. Game and puzzle-quiz ideas are followed by examples to show how they may be used in the classroom. With these examples as starting points, the ideas may be changed, enlarged, or otherwise altered to fit any ability range for any age group.

This volume is not a course of study nor is it a textbook. It is intended to serve as a supplement, a practical guide, a point of departure. The material presented is a beginning rather than an end, and it can help make social studies an enjoyable experience for both student and teacher.

This collection provides enrichment activities which have been used in a variety of situations and found to be successful and rewarding. The materials are presented alphabetically to serve as a ready reference, a source of reliable enrichment activities that can be adapted to various situations. In practice, certain activities will emerge as student favorites and become standard fare for future years.

Don't be reluctant to alter any of the games or activities to fit your class. There is nothing sacred about any of them. From time to time, an activity is suggested for use with students at a certain level. This does not mean that the activity can't be used at any other level. Such suggestions are intended only as a guide for the busy teacher. There is virtually no idea which can't be modified so that it is valuable at any level. In general, most activities included may, with some modifications, be used at any level from grades six through twelve.

The key to success in using this material is knowing your class. That is the beginning point for the use of any enrichment material.

■ GAMES

Young people generally enjoy playing games. The thrill of competition adds to the enjoyment. Students in social studies classes are no exception—they enjoy games and can profit from the learning or review achieved through playing the game.

Many of the games which follow are old favorites adapted especially for the social studies classroom. Others have been designed especially for classroom use. Some allow students to compete on an individual basis with one another, while others foster group cooperation as one group competes with another. Still others allow the student to compete against himself or against a given standard. All the games work with students, though not all games are suitable for a given class.

Many of the games require pencil and paper responses, others involve oral participation. Some involve preparation of special charts, cards, and the like. However, such preparation is usually on a one-time basis, and the resultant materials can be reused for years. The time spent in initial preparation isn't overly prohibitive when spread over the life of the game.

Don't limit your game activities to those included in this section. Develop game ideas on your own and encourage the students to do the same. Many commercial games are useful to the social studies teacher and more are coming out every year. Use the good ones when you can.

The games that follow often include an illustrative example to help clarify the organization of the game. Be sure you understand how the game functions before presenting it to the class. Go through a "dry run" at home.

No one game is best for all classes and purposes. Some will prove more popular than others with your students. Children like old friends whether they be people, books, or games. Games are excellent devices for use at interest centers, for class reviews, for spare moments, and for directed study. Don't, however, forget that the games, while fun, are learning activities. If no learning accompanies the game, both you and your students lose.

Affinities

■ Some things go together such as Dagwood and Blondie, pork and beans, or bow and arrow. History is full of such affinities or pairs and from these you can construct an interesting contest.

The most obvious use of affinities is for the players to make individual or team lists of affinities from history. The winning individual or team is, of course, the one which compiles the longest list in a given time.

A second way to use affinities for class contests is for the teacher to compile a fairly lengthy list of affinities prior to class. The list is then divided so that one part of the affinity is separated from the second. The second list is then scrambled so the students are presented with the affinities on two separate lists. The contest involves the rematching of the affinities into correct pairs.

Affinities may be used nicely for an oral game in which the class is divided into two teams. The first player from team A gives the first part of the affinity. The first player from team B completes the affinity by giving the second half. If he is unsuccessful, team A gets one point and the next player on team B is asked to supply the missing half of the affinity. If he answers correctly, he then gives the first half of a new affinity for the next player on team A in turn to add to. This procedure continues until time runs out or a predetermined score has been reached.

In any game of affinities, keep in mind that there may be several possible ways to complete a pair. For example, Antony is the obvious affinity for Cleopatra, but Egypt might also be acceptable.

An oral game of affinities might proceed like this.

Team A, player one:	Tigris River.
Team B, player one:	Euphrates. Antony.
Team A, player two:	Cleopatra. Sword.
Team B, player two:	Shield. Bow.
Team A, player three:	Arrow. Zeus.
Team B, player three:	Hera. Circus.
Team A, player four:	I don't know. (*score 1 point for Team B*)
Team A, player five:	Gladiator. Circus.
Team B, player four:	Chariot race. Catacombs.
Team A, player six:	Christians. Gaul.

And so on around the group.

It goes without saying that no student may supply the first half of an affinity unless he has a second half in mind. Be sure the players understand this before the game begins.

Animal, Vegetable, or Mineral

■ The quiz game of Animal, Vegetable, or Mineral has been a standby of teachers for years. In this game, perhaps better known as Twenty Questions, a leader selects a subject. He then tells the group which of the three categories the subject belongs in: animal, vegetable, or mineral. It is then up to the group to identify the subject by questioning the leader who may answer only with a "yes" or a "no." The student who is finally successful in identifying the secret subject becomes leader for the next game and chooses his own subject. Should the group be unable to learn the identity of the subject within twenty questions, the leader wins and either gives a new subject or appoints a leader for the next game.

Good students delight in the test of wits required to identify the subject in the required twenty questions. Even less able students get into the swing of things though their questions may not be quite so discriminating as those of the more able players.

With larger groups, allow questioning in random order. Small groups may desire to ask questions in rotation. This should be up to the group, though random questioning usually works best.

The game might go like this when the subject is Henry VIII.

Leader:	The subject is animal.
Question one:	Is it a man?

Leader:	Yes.
Question two:	Is he living?
Leader:	No.
Question three:	Was he a general?
Leader:	No.
Question four:	Was he a ruler?
Leader:	Yes.
Question five:	Did he rule in Europe?
Leader:	Yes.
Question six:	Did he rule France?
Leader:	No.
Question seven:	Did he rule Russia?
Leader:	No.
Question eight:	Did he rule England?
Leader:	Yes.

And so on until either Henry VIII is guessed or the group uses the twenty questions allowed.

This quiz game is an excellent classroom activity. A single round can be played in a few minutes, or a series can take a fairly long period of time. The action is quick, so the players are not likely to get bored.

Answer My Question

■ Every class has a few students who delight in stumping their fellow students and even the teacher from time to time. This game is tailor-made for these students.

It is essentially a team quiz game. There is a basic difference, however, which makes it a bit better than the ordinary quiz game. In this game the team decides on the difficulty of each question and assigns it a point value according to its difficulty. Questions are rated with a score from 1 to 5, with harder questions receiving the higher rating. The other team is then allowed five tries in which they attempt to correctly answer the question. A student who successfully answers the question receives the allotted number of points regardless of whether his answer is the first, second, or even fifth. In addition the player who supplies the correct answer becomes the new questioner.

If, however, the players are unable to supply the required

answer in the allotted five questions, the leader scores the points for himself and asks a new question.

The game goes like this.

Team A, player one:	For 2 points, can you tell me who developed the alphabet we use today?
Team B, player one:	The Greeks?
Team A, player one:	No.
Team B, player two:	The Romans?
Team A, player one:	No.
Team B, player three:	The Egyptians?
Team A, player one:	No.
Team B, player four:	The Phoenicians?
Team A, player one:	Correct. Team B scores 2 points.
Team B, player four:	*(asks new question)*

The game ends when a predetermined score or time limit has been reached.

Bingo

■ History Bingo games are tops with students. This is especially true of students of junior high age. The game has the advantage of being familiar to students, so virtually no explanation is necessary. Initial preparation, however, takes considerable time, though it is well worth the effort spent.

Always prepare enough student playing cards so there are extras. A student with no success is likely to want to exchange his "unlucky" card for one with more "luck."

In setting up the game establish definite historic limits for the questions. For example, a good Bingo game might cover ancient Greece and Rome. Another might deal with the development of modern Europe. Once the period to be covered by a given game is decided upon, the next step is preparing the questions. Write or type each question on a small, stiff card. The answer goes on the back. These cards can be shuffled following each game so that the questions for the next game are in different order. Fifty questions for each game provide a variety of information for review, yet allow each student to have one answer for every other question since student cards contain twenty-four answers.

When the questions have been decided upon and written on cards, set up the student playing cards. Again use stiff stock for the cards. No two student playing cards can be the same. Each card will contain answers to about half the possible questions, but these answers will be in differing locations from card to card. No card will have the same set of answers as another and the answers will change position from one card to the next.

These instructions outline the procedure for a teacher-made game. Do not, however, overlook the value of having students prepare the questions and the game boards. Some of the best and longest-lasting learning comes from just such assignments.

Use Bingo games for small groups or for class size contests. Traditionally, the winner becomes the caller for the next game. Buttons make good counters for Bingo, though corn kernels, small plastic discs, or cardboard markers work about as well. Be sure not to use lightweight paper for markers. It is hard to handle and has a tendency to blow off cards.

Though the suggestion is possibly unnecessary, always have the winning player read back his answers before being declared the winner. Even the best intentioned player will slip up from time to time.

The following illustrations show how we might set up a Bingo game covering ancient Greece and Rome. The eight questions given deal only with Greece. Four cards are shown to give the teacher an idea of how answers might be distributed among the cards. Note that each card has answers to only half the questions, that the answers appear in scrambled position from card to card, and that the answers to the same questions don't appear on the same cards. The answers should be scrambled as completely as possible. The first player who can cover a row of five answers vertically, horizontally, or diagonally has "bingo."

Note, too, that the student playing cards have the upper right-hand corner clipped. This allows the cards to be quickly arranged so that each card is face up and right side up. Also, it allows use of the backs of the cards for a second game. The clipped corner makes sure no student tries to use the wrong side of the card when both sides are used. Simply direct the students to have the clipped corner at the upper right or upper left and the game is ready to go. The same system on the question cards makes them easy to sort, with questions face up and answers face down.

Sample questions for Bingo might include the following ones. (For sample student playing cards, see Figure 1.)

1

Zeus	Colosseum	Pericles	Delian League	Virgil
Thermopylae	Senate	Brutus	**Solon**	Cato
Augustus	Council		Circus	Syracuse
Patrician	**Sparta**	Salamis	Carthage	Alexander
Aristotle	Romulus	Darius	Tribune	**Draco**

2

Virgil	Macedonia	Gaul	Persia	Cato
Delian League	Marathon	Carthage	**Athens**	Philip
Plato	Consuls		Syracuse	Plebeian
Hera	Socrates	**Acropolis**	Darius	Circus
Thermopylae	Zeus	Forum	Bucephalus	Pompey

Figure 1. Four student playing cards for Bingo. (Bold type is used here to show answers to questions on page 11. Of course, in the actual game, counters or markers would cover the answers.) *Continued on page 10.*

3

Hannibal	Persia	Plebeian	Remus	Olympus
Democracy	Bucephalus	Philip	**Plato**	Augustus
Cleon	Pericles		Socrates	Forum
Republic	**Draco**	Romulus	Assembly	Pompey
Acropolis	Colosseum	Caesar	Senate	Homer

4

Marathon	Brutus	Consuls	**Sparta**	Hannibal
Caesar	Salamis	Remus	Republic	Alexander
Athens	Aristotle		Cleon	**Solon**
Assembly	Macedonia	Tribune	Council	Gaul
Olympus	Patrician	**Democracy**	Homer	Hera

Figure 1 (continued)

1. Six thousand Spartans faced about one hundred eighty thousand Persians in a losing battle at a mountain pass. Where was this battle? (Thermopylae)
2. What Greek required the laws to be written so all could know their rights? (Draco)
3. What form of government had its beginnings in Greece? (democracy)
4. What Greek city-state was known for its war-like attitude and military preparedness? (Sparta)
5. Which Greek city-state is remembered for its democratic form of government? (Athens)
6. Which Greek made it unlawful for a person to be sold into slavery because of debts he owed? (Solon)
7. Which Greek writer wrote a plan for a perfect nation in his book *The Republic?* (Plato)
8. Athena's temple was built atop what famous hill in Athens? (Acropolis)

Categories

■ Here is a fast-moving game which requires absolutely no preparation and can be played any time and any place. It is a progressive game in which no player remains leader for more than a few seconds at a time.

To open the game, name a subject or category. The first player who can give an answer to match the chosen category calls out his answer. He scores a point for himself and immediately names a category for the other players. It may be the same category for which he just supplied an answer or it may be a new category. A category may be repeated any number of times in the game but no answer may be used more than once for any one category. If an answer fits more than one category it may be used more than once, but each time for different categories.

At the end of the period of play the student who has scored the most points is declared winner.

A variation of the game of Categories is played in rotation about the room. The first student supplies a category and the next student is expected to supply an answer. If he does so, he gains a point and names a category for the next student. If he fails, he gains no point and play moves to the next student with the category already given. After the play has gone around the group a number of times the student with the most correct answers and, consequently, the most points is declared winner. In case of a tie, those students with the greatest number of points may have a tie-breaking contest among themselves.

The game, as first described, goes along in this fashion.

First player:	The category is continents.
Player:	Asia. Next category bodies of water.
Player:	Indian Ocean. Next category rivers.
Player:	Mekong. Next category islands.
Player:	Ceylon. Next category mountain ranges.
Player:	Himalaya. Next category continents.
Player:	Africa. Next category ...

And so goes the game. Note the repeated category of continents.

This game is extremely fast when played with older students of similar abilities. Everyone must stay on his toes or get left far behind. It can be used time after time without getting stale and is a new game with every playing. There is no time limit. It can run from a minute to as long as student interest holds out.

Charades

■ The old game of Charades has been used for parties, youth gatherings, and drama classes for years. These uses don't prevent it from being a useful game for the social studies class. Charades in the social studies class may be a spur of the moment sort of thing or a bit more formal with the players given time to work out their ideas before class presentation.

In Charades, players attempt to act out an event from history without words but in such a manner as to allow other members of the class to guess the event portrayed. For this reason the action needs to be vivid, even exaggerated. The students with a flair for the dramatic will relish this and throw their entire being into the performance.

Whether a charade requires one student or several depends on the subject chosen. When several students are involved the group should have a moment or two to prepare their charade even when presentations are of an impromptu nature.

Though historic events are standard fare for the charade performers, don't overlook the possibilities offered by the lives of the great and interesting from history. Instead of having a complete charade presented before allowing the other students to attempt to identify the event enacted, the performer or performers present one event in the life of the person they have chosen. Then the other players are allowed to attempt identification of the character the actors have in mind. If the group is unsuccessful, another event is presented in charade form. This continues with guesses and charade alternating until some student is successful in identifying the character represented by the series of charades. This successful player presents the next charade with the help of other class members of his choosing.

Students should have no difficulty in coming up with historic happenings and characters they wish to deal with in charade. In case ideas are needed, try the following historic events in your class.

> The discovery of fire
> Moses leading the flight from Egypt
> A Roman circus
> Cortez conquering the Aztecs in Mexico
> The American Revolution
> Invention of movable type and the printing press
> The assassination of Abraham Lincoln
> Perry's opening of Japan to the West

For the lives of the great try some of these names.

Michelangelo	Galileo
Martin Luther	Edward Jenner
Christopher Columbus	Mohandas Gandhi
Henry VIII	Charles de Gaulle
Isaac Newton	

Dates

■ This little game may be used as an oral activity or a pencil and paper contest. It is a good time-filler for a few odd moments. Divide the class into two or more teams of equal numbers. The teacher or leader gives the group a date from history. This date might be a year when dealing with modern or contemporary history or a century or historic period when dealing with less recent history. The object of the game is for each player to name or write an event from history which occurred during the time assigned. To score the game, give each pupil 1 point for his team for each correct event he supplies.

Dialogues

■ This game is an historic charade with words. The object is to identify two (or more) students who are playing the parts of a noted historic team. The actors carry on a conversation with one another, dropping clues to their historic identity. The other players attempt to determine the identity the speakers have assumed. The first student to make a correct identification chooses one or more partners and they become the next historic characters to carry on a dialogue.

To keep the game going, the speakers must constantly drop hints to their identity in their speech. These hints may refer to the history of the time in which the characters lived, to individuals who would have lived at the same time in history, or events in the lives of the characters speaking. The speakers should stop at regular intervals to enable the others to attempt to guess their historic identity.

It is often a good idea to have students choose partners and decide beforehand on the characters they wish to impersonate so they can do some research. Though actual rehearsal isn't a good idea, some thought should be given to the clues the group will give the class.

Whenever possible it is a good plan to have all characters in the dialogue represent famous persons. Noted pairs such as Antony and Cleopatra are great but fairly hard to come by. Churchill and Roosevelt are a valid pair though they aren't usually thought of as a pair. It is also acceptable to have only one character to identify—for example, San Martin talking to a Latin revolutionary—so long as the observers are informed in advance which actor represents the player whose identity they have to guess.

Dialogues allow for the creative touch on the part of clever students. A crafty team can drop clues all over the place yet manage to conceal their identity for quite a time. It also lets students stand before the class in an informal situation. For some, this is a boon.

Dialogues provide for some good research when students really prepare for them. With or without prior research, Dialogues are fun for both speakers and listeners. Try them and see.

Discussion

■ Discussion is a simple exercise in extemporaneous speaking. It isn't the sort of thing you would wish to do every day but as an entertaining fill-in, it is lots of fun and serves to keep the students on their toes.

Two students participate in a discussion. They stand facing each other and discuss a topic assigned to them. The idea is for one student to begin the discussion and the other to carry it on when the first stops talking. This continues in rotation until the time limit for the discussion is reached.

What determines when one student stops talking and the other starts? The students themselves do. The instant the speaker pauses noticeably the other must at once begin speaking. Neither can repeat a fact or idea stated by the other.

This little contest is far harder than it might appear at first glance so keep the time limit short until you see how it goes.

For starters, consider giving the student topics similar to the following suggestions for this activity.

> Why I would have liked to be in the army of Alexander the Great
> Why I would not have enjoyed being a citizen of Sparta
> Why I would rather live today than during the Middle Ages
> What I would have done had I been a member of Columbus' crew
> How I would have changed things if I had been Peter the Great

Extempore

■ Do you have a student who, without exception, is always engaged in speaking, whether the speech is a monologue, a dialogue, or totally a monopoly? Who doesn't have one such student! Extempore is just the game for such a member of the class.

Extempore is just what the name implies — an unrehearsed speech before the group. Choose the student (victim?) and present him with a topic. Allow five seconds for preparation. Any break in the flow of words during the next sixty seconds can't be longer than a count of three. A violation of the three count retires the speaker. You may wish to keep track of the amount of time each speaker is able to keep going. This could be a good filler for time remaining at the end of a period or on a Monday morning to wake everyone up after the weekend.

Extempore is to be used sparingly. It calls for some fairly serious research if valid historic topics are assigned. On the other hand it can bring down the house if the topics assigned allow a clever and talkative student a bit of historic fun. Ideas which can lead to merriment further enliven the game, such as

> I cared for Hannibal's elephants
> My adventures teaching George I to speak English
> My first month as a stamp seller in Colonial America

We don't intend to make light of history, just to enjoy teaching it. A little historic spoof now and then won't spoil history for the students, and it may cause them to start looking for the human and often amusing side of history.

Fast Talk

■ In this fast-moving game of recall and association, the object is to keep from being the leader or "it." The player who is "it" constantly attempts to relinquish his dubious position to another player. He does this by naming an historic character, pointing at another player, and counting from one to ten at a fairly rapid clip. The player pointed at must supply a fact about the character named before whoever is "it" reaches ten in his counting. If he is successful, the player who is "it" seeks another victim. If the player put on the spot is slow in coming forth with a correct fact or gives an incorrect answer, he replaces "it" and goes in search of another victim.

A no-repeat rule is used which forbids repeating a fact. However, the same historic individual or location may be used a number of times. Also, a person who has just given a correct answer may well be put on the spot immediately by "it."

Here is how the game might go.

It:	Winston Churchill. (*begins counting*)
Player indicated:	Prime minister.
It:	Charles de Gaulle (*begins counting*)
Player indicated:	French.
It:	Winston Churchill. (*begins counting*)
Player indicated:	Smoked cigars.
It:	Joseph Stalin (*begins counting*)
Player indicated:	Russian leader.
It:	Winston Churchill. (*begins counting*)
Player indicated:	Went to Yalta.
It:	Franklin Roosevelt (*begins counting*)
Player indicated:	Attended Potsdam Conference.
It:	Wrong answer. Truman went to Potsdam.

The unfortunate player who gave the wrong answer is the new "it" and the game goes wildly on.

Flash Cards

■ The use of flash cards in math and reading is commonplace. Using them in history isn't nearly so common, but it can be just as successful as in the other subjects.

A flash card needs to be lettered large enough to allow easy reading at a distance of several feet. This limits the length of the question or requires a flash card of considerable size. Rather than use oversized cards, it is better to settle for shorter questions.

On the back of each card is the answer to the question appearing on the face. This enables the individual flashing the question to have the answer before him without having to see the face of the card.

Flash cards can be used best in small groups. They are primarily a review technique, as the answer must be previously known. Teams compete with one another to give the correct answer in the shortest possible time. Thus, flash cards are usually used as a contest form.

Keep score by having the team who gives the correct answer

first collect the card. At the end of the contest the team holding the greatest number of cards wins the contest.

Students can make their own flash cards for team use. A fairly stiff stock is best for construction. Black Magic Marker shows up well for the lettering. Clip off the upper right-hand corner of each card. This allows easy sorting of flash cards so that all are right side up and the questions all face up.

A good twist is to reverse the flash cards from time to time and show the answers. The object then, of course, is to supply the question which would have led to the answer given.

Flash cards are popular items at an interest center or an activity corner. Generally, such use is restricted to younger social studies students. Few high-school age students will use them in this fashion, though there are always exceptions.

Football

■ The use of a football field layout is a popular game form for social studies students. The game as played has nothing to do with athletic football. The field layout is merely a score-keeping device that can be used with any set of questions. Though the game can be used with class-size groups, it is far better as a small group or pairs activity.

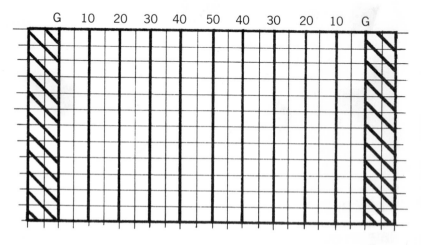

Figure 2. The arrangement of a field in the game of Football.

To begin the game a football field layout is needed, drawn on a fairly large sheet of oaktag (see diagram in Figure 2). If individuals will be playing in pairs, a 9″ × 12″ sheet will do nicely. Small groups will probably do better with a little larger field. Should the game be used for an entire class, a playing field perhaps 24″ × 48″ or even larger is needed so those at the rear of the room can see where the play is.

Pairs and small groups can use an eraser to keep track of the "ball" movements. Larger groups will find a strip of colored paper attached to the upper edge of the playing field with a paper clip an ideal "ball."

The group is divided into two teams. Play begins with the receiving team or offense placing the ball on its own 20-yard line. The defense gives the offense a quiz question. If the team correctly answers the question, the ball is moved forward 10 yards, placing it on the 30-yard line. This continues until the offense fails to answer a question or reaches the goal line.

When a question is missed, the ball does not move, but the opposing team takes possession and begins receiving questions to answer and the ball moves in the opposite direction.

Any time a team reaches the goal line, it receives 6 points. After a goal is scored, the team making the score receives one more question for the extra point. If it is answered correctly, the team scores an additional point. After a touchdown and extra point try, the ball is moved to the other team's 20-yard line where the opposing side takes possession and starts answering questions.

A good variation of the contest requires that each side rate their questions according to difficulty. The questions are placed in three classes: easy, medium, and difficult. The team with the ball then requests questions by type. An easy question correctly answered moves the ball forward 10 yards. Medium questions gain 20 yards, and difficult questions are worth 30 yards. A missed question causes the ball to remain where it is and change hands, just as in the first form of the game.

Guess My Name

■ In this game, one student asks members of the class to guess the name of an historic character or geographic location. To help the students learn the identity of the character or location, the leader gives clues from time to time. A new clue after every two or three incorrect guesses helps keep the game moving and maintains player interest. The player who is successful in guessing the identity of the character or location becomes leader for the next round.

Since the leader gives continuous clues about the identity of the unknown person or location, the players may not ask leading questions. They may only give the names of individuals they think fit the clues given them by the leader.

The game might go like this.

Leader:	I'm a capital city. Guess my name.
Player:	Are you in North America?
Leader:	No.
Player:	Are you in South America?
Leader:	No. I am in the Eastern Hemisphere.
Player:	Are you in Russia?
Leader:	No.
Player:	Are you in Germany?
Leader:	No. I am near water.

The questioning continues until London is arrived at in this example. The successful player becomes the next leader and a new game begins.

Guggenheim

■ Here is a pencil and paper game with the improbable name of Guggenheim. Teachers, youth leaders, and families have been playing this little game for generations.

Guggenheim may be played by any number of players. It has a limitless number of possible solutions which change with every game played. The game makes use of a number of categories and a lead or beginning word. The categories are listed along the left-hand side of the playing paper and the key or game word is written across the top. (See the Guggenheim chart shown.)

Key words of four or five letters are enough for a short game. Usually it is a good idea to choose words in which no letter is repeated, though this does not have to be the case. If a word with a double or repeated letter is used, then different entries are required for the answers for these letters. Five or six categories provide enough variety for a good game, though the number is up to the group. A dozen or more categories could be used for a fairly long game.

Play begins with each player attempting to give one word for each category. The words used begin with the letters shown at the top of the game in the beginning word. A time limit is set and play begins. Each player fills in the Guggenheim chart as rapidly as possible. The winner is the player who, at the end of the allotted time, has filled the most spaces correctly.

Guggenheim may be played by individuals, pairs, or even teams. It is sometimes a good idea to allow the players to choose the categories they wish to use. At other times, the teacher may wish to specify categories. Each new game requires a new key word so that each game is entirely different from the previous one.

The possible categories are unlimited in Guggenheim. This allows it to be used again and again without growing old.

The Guggenheim chart given in Figure 3 has been partly filled in to indicate how the game goes. The key word was *help*, as can be seen at the top of the chart.

Categories	H	E	L	P
Military Leader	Hannibal			
King			Louis XIV	
Weapon			Lance	
Famous Woman	Helen			
Religious Leader			Luther	
Pope				Paul

Figure 3. An example of a chart used in a game of Guggenheim.

From time to time you may wish to allow the players to fill in any number of answers for a given category and letter. For example, in the above chart using the category Pope and the letter P, a player could add Pius and Peter to the list thus increasing his score.

Hangman

■ Doubtless you have played Hangman. Have you ever used it with your social studies class? It is an excellent game for pairs of students, for small groups, and for the entire class as an odd-moment filler.

The game begins with the leader drawing a gallows and placing a series of dashes under it to represent the letters in a word or phrase to be guessed by the group (see Figure 4). The players are

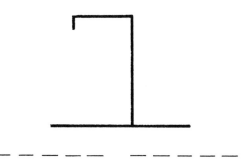

Figure 4. An example of a diagram to be completed
for a two-word game of Hangman.

now ready to attempt to guess the word(s) beneath the gallows. This is done letter by letter until the word(s) are spelled out or until a student is ready to give the word(s) from the letters already present. Each time a student guesses a correct letter that letter is placed in the appropriate blank, or blanks if the letter appears more than one time. Each time an incorrect letter is given, a member of the hangman is drawn. (This also holds true when a student tries for the entire word and guesses incorrectly—the penalty is still only a single member of the hangman.)

The hangman is made of seven pieces: head, neck, body, two arms, and two legs. If the entire hangman is completed before the word(s) are guessed, the leader wins. If a player completes the word(s) first, the players win.

In the history class, each word or phrase used must refer to a given period in history. This may be the historic period under current study or one previously studied. The leader may fill in one letter or not as class policy dictates, though that letter need not be the beginning letter. When the missing word(s) contain the same letter more than once, it is customary to fill in all blanks containing that letter if it is guessed—though older students may wish to make the game harder by filling only one slot at a time, forcing players to search for repeated letters. Make sure the ground rules are clear before play begins.

A standard game of Hangman for a class studying documents of human rights or thirteenth-century England might be as follows.

First guess:	Is there an *e*?
Leader:	No. (*head is drawn*)
Second guess:	Is there an *o*?
Leader:	No. (*neck is drawn*)
Third guess:	Is there an *a*?
Leader:	Yes. (*four a's are placed in blanks*)
Fourth guess:	Is there an *i*?
Leader:	No. (*body is drawn*)
Fifth guess:	Is there an *l*?
Leader:	No. (*an arm is drawn*)
Sixth guess:	Is there a *c*?
Leader:	Yes. (*the c is placed in its blank*)
Seventh guess:	Is there an *r*?
Leader:	Yes. (*the r is placed*)

The Hangman diagram now looks like the one shown in Figure 5.

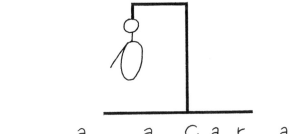

Figure 5.   _ a _ _ a c a r _ a

The players should get *Magna Carta* before losing the game.

A good variation of this game requires guessing the entire word or phrase without spelling it letter by letter. Again, the given period in history is set and a blank or blanks are shown to indicate the number of words the players are hunting.

Before each guess, however, a clue is given as to the identity of the missing word(s).

A game might go like this when the Middle Ages were under study and there is only one blank indicated.

Clue:	This came during the Middle Ages.
First guess:	Crusades?

Answer and clue:	No. (*head is drawn*) It involves trade.
Second guess:	Is it cities?
Answer and clue:	No. (*the neck is drawn*) It helped traders.
Third guess:	Roads?
Answer and clue:	No. (*the body is drawn*) Traders used this in cities.
Fourth guess:	Fairs?
Answer and clue:	No. (*an arm is drawn*) It helped make trading easier and safer.
Fifth guess:	Laws?
Answer and clue:	No. (*the second arm is drawn*) It had to do with money.
Sixth guess:	Banking?
Answer:	Yes.

The student giving the correct answer now becomes leader for the next game.

Heroes

■ The game of Heroes is enjoyed by students in early junior high. It is a question and answer type game in which the players eventually discover the identity of a hero through questions they ask the game leader.

Play begins with the leader declaring he is thinking of a hero. Players may then ask questions which may be answered either "yes" or "no" by the leader. These may be questions designed to give clues to the identity of the hero under discussion or may be possible answers for the name of the hero.

Play ends when a student is successful in stating the hero's identity.

Heroes goes like this.

Leader:	I'm thinking of a hero.
Player:	Was he a president?
Leader:	No.
Player:	Was he a dictator?
Leader:	No.
Player:	Was he a general?
Leader:	Yes.

Player:	Was he an English general?
Leader:	No.
Player:	Was he French?
Leader:	No.
Player:	Was he American?
Leader:	Yes.
Player:	Is he still alive?
Leader:	No.
Player:	Did he fight in the Revolutionary War?
Leader:	No.
Player:	Was he in the Civil War?
Leader:	Yes.
Player:	Did he fight for the North?
Leader:	No.
Player:	Was he Robert E. Lee?
Leader:	No.

Questions and answers go on until J. E. B. Stuart is identified. Then a new hero is selected and the game begins anew. This is a really fine question and answer game for younger players who are interested in the greats from history. They will ask to play it again and again. After playing it in class a time or two, don't be surprised when students come to you and confide they have a great hero in mind which is sure to fool the class next time they play the game.

Historic Location

■ A tremendous number of events from history, items of historic significance, and biographical bits of information are directly related to a specific locale—a country or a city.

In this game, the leader states a fact from history, for example, a given event, the happening in the life of an individual, or merely the name of some item of historic importance. The other players are then faced with the task of relating it to a city or nation. The first student to give the correct relationship receives a point and becomes the new leader. For each player who can't give the correct relationship, the leader scores a point for himself. The person who finally identifies the relationship scores a point and assumes the role of leader.

The game is played like this.

Player A (leader):	What city is related to the last battle in the War of 1812?
Player B:	Washington, D.C.?
Leader:	No.
Player C:	New Orleans?
Player A:	Right.
Player C (new leader):	What city is related to the deaths of generals Montcalm and Wolfe?
Player D:	Toronto?
Player C:	No.
Player E:	Quebec?
Player C:	Right.

SCORING: Player A—1 point; player C—2 points; player E—1 point.

History from A to Z

■ In History from A to Z individuals, pairs, or teams compete against one another in listing events, individuals, etc., from history. Each player or team letters a column from A to Z. In a given time frame, they list items beginning with A to fill as many of the slots as they can. Only one item may be entered per letter. In other words, no credit is given for multiple answers for any given letter.

When time is called, the player or team which has most nearly completed the alphabetical list is the winner. This isn't a game you want to use too often, but from time to time it is a good refresher. Possible categories might include military leaders, heads of state, explorers, ancient Greece, the Civil War, and leaders of World War II.

I Know a Person

■ Even the youngest history students can play this game and be successful at it. It is a fast-moving question and answer game dealing with historic personages.

Play begins with the leader telling the group, "I know a person whose name begins with the letter _." The other players then try to guess who the leader has in mind. The one who succeeds in identifying the person the leader has in mind becomes leader for the next round.

After three or four unsuccessful guesses, the leader gives the players a clue which should help them identify the mystery person. These clues, coupled with the letter of the individual's last name or commonly used name, will eventually result in a correct identification.

Play might go like this.

Leader:	I know a person whose name begins with the letter P.
Player:	Is it King Philip?
Leader:	No.
Player:	Is it Prince Henry the Navigator?
Leader:	No.
Player:	Is it anyone named Philip?
Leader:	No. The letter P begins his nast name.
Player:	Is it Admiral Porter?
Leader:	No.
Player:	Is it William Pitt?
Leader:	No.
Player:	Is it Franklin Pierce?
Leader:	No. He was an early explorer.
Player:	Is it Marco Polo?
Leader:	Yes, it is.

The successful player is the new leader and another round begins at once.

This game can be expanded to include places and events from history as well as inventions, ideas, and any other category of historic importance.

Try this one with the younger historians (and even the older ones for that matter), and it will be demanded again and again.

It Looks Familiar

■ Here is a review game with a different twist which has proven quite interesting. It does require a bit of preparation before play can begin. This preparation consists of locating and mounting pictures, drawings, paintings, or sketches of famous people from history, noted historic events, or places of historic significance.

Once these pictures are mounted and assembled, play may begin. The game or contest consists of displaying one item and asking for answers concerning the picture shown.

The class is divided into two or more teams of equal size. Each player keeps a numbered score sheet on which he records his responses. At the end of a dozen or so questions, the answers are checked. The team with the highest total of correct responses wins.

The questions asked may go from picture to picture or a number of questions concerning one illustration may be asked. Pictures might be displayed one at a time for identification of the name of the person pictured, the historic event shown, or perhaps the location of the item pictured.

On the other hand, a picture of Julius Caesar might be displayed and half a dozen questions asked about that picture before a second picture is used. The questions might go as follows for Julius Caesar.

1. Who is this man?
2. Where did he live?
3. When in history was he important?
4. What were two of his military conquests?
5. How was he important politically?
6. What romantic interest did he have?
7. How did he die?

This game is an excellent change of pace. The preparation may require a bit of searching, but once a good illustration has been found and mounted, it can be used again and again.

Jeopardy

■ The quiz game of Jeopardy is possibly the finest of all games for the social studies classroom. The game to which we refer is a teacher-constructed version of the commercial game by the same name.

The game is played with a series of categories and a number of questions dealing with each category. Usually four or five categories give the game sufficient variety, with anywhere from five to ten questions per category supplying enough depth to make an activity of reasonable length.

Preparation involves selection of the categories and writing of the questions for the selected categories. Question-writing is a good student activity. Categories of people, places, things, and ideas prove a great range of learning and will be useful in game after game.

In writing the questions for any given category, try to constuct questions of varying difficulty. Point values can then be assigned to the questions. Thus, easy questions are worth 5 points, more difficult ones are worth 10 points, and the really tough ones go for 15 points.

Once the questions have been written and values assigned, the game of Jeopardy is ready to be played. It works well as a small group activity and almost as well in larger groups. In small groups, individuals play independently. Larger groups divide into teams.

When a question is asked, the first player to raise his hand following the reading of the question is allowed to answer. If his answer is correct, he scores the point value of the question. Should the answer prove wrong, the point value is subtracted from his or his team's score. In play the game goes like this for World War I.

Student A:	I'd like a 5-point question on people.
Leader:	Who was leader of the A.E.F.?
Student B:	General Pershing.

The correct answer scores 5 points. That student picks the next category and point value.

Student B:	I'd like a 15-point question from ideas.
Leader:	What foreign affairs policy was followed by Americans after World War I?
Student C:	Isolationism.

This answer scores 15 points and the student giving it picks the next category and point value.

Student C:	I'd like a 5 pointer from places.
Leader:	The Germans invaded what country in order to reach France?
Student D:	Spain.

This incorrect answer loses 5 points. At this point the moderator (probably the teacher) must be sharp of eye for the second hand up is now in line to answer.

Student A:	Belgium.

Five points are scored and the game continues.

It is usually a good idea to note the categories on the board for easy reference by players. Also, if no hand goes up for a given question, allow the student calling for that question to give another category and point value.

This is a popular game and can be played often without becoming stale.

Lives of the Great

■ Teams prepare for this game by assembling clues to the identity of great persons. These clues are arranged in groups of five for each individual. Ideally, the first clue or two should deal with an obscure bit of information or even be accurate but misleading, if at all possible. The later clues should be more specific and easier to associate with the person to whom they refer.

When the game begins, the questioner reads the clues one at a time. Following each clue, the opposing team is allowed one guess for the identity of the person in question. The first guess is worth 5 points, if it produces a correct answer. The guess after the second clue is worth 4 points, and so on until the fifth and final guess, which is worth only 1 point. A set of clues which stumps the opposing team gives the questioning team 10 points. When one round is completed, the roles switch, so the questioners become the questioned.

This can be a pencil and paper game involving a large group or the whole class. The leader reads the clues slowly, one at a time. After the reading of every clue, each player writes a guess. When the fifth clue is read, the correct identification is given. Each player records his own score, and his score will depend upon the point at which he made the proper identification. When a student is certain he has correctly identified the character in question, he repeats the same answer for the next statements or uses ditto marks to indicate his satisfaction with his choice of answer. Team scores are totaled from each player's responses.

Here is a sample round.

Team I:	His first name was Vladimir.
Team II:	Stalin?
Team I:	No. He was once sent to Siberia.
Team II:	Karl Marx?
Team I:	No. He took part in the 1917 Revolution.

Team II:	Trotsky?
Team I:	No. He was the father of Russian Communism.
Team II:	Lenin?
Team I:	Right.

Team II scored 2 points by correctly identifying Lenin on the fourth question.

Names

■ As the title might suggest, this is a game in which players are called upon to supply names. It is most generally played as a pencil and paper game in which each student lists names on his own. It works equally well as a team game in which small teams work together to compile lists of names. It can be used as an oral game in which players supply names in rotation.

As with many such games, there are several good variations of Names. Players are given a category such as battles, rulers, military men, or the like. They then supply as many names as possible to match the category.

A second variation requires the players to supply names important to history beginning with a given letter of the alphabet. When Names is played in this fashion, any name of historic importance is accepted so long as it begins with the letter designated. Each separate contest uses a different letter, of course.

If Names is played orally, each student supplying a name in his turn receives a point for his team and each one failing to give a name loses a point.

When pencil and paper listing is used, the team compiling the most points is winner of that game. It is a good idea to keep the games rather short and move from category to category fairly rapidly.

Quotable Quotes

■ Historic quotations have a definite place in the social studies classroom. They quite often provide insights into the thinking that took place during a given historic period. This classroom game uses quotations to provide quick historic review.

The leader reads a quotation to the other players. They then try to identify the individual who made the statement. When a player incorrectly identifies the source of a quotation, the leader gives the players a clue to the identity of the speaker, to the historic period in which he lived, or some fact that might lead to the identification of the quoted individual.

The student who successfully identifies the speaker becomes the next leader and then gives a quote and clues of his own. For this reason every player needs to prepare several quotations and clues prior to the beginning of play. *Bartlett's Familiar Quotations* or a comparable book should be available to the students in every social studies class for this activity and others.

The game is played in this manner.

Leader: "Dictators ride to and fro upon tigers which they dare not dismount. And the tigers are getting hungry." Who said this?

Player: Was it Franklin Roosevelt?

Leader: No. He is famous as a writer.

Player: Was it Dumas?

Leader: No. He fought in India.

Player: Was it Alexander the Great?

Leader: No. He was once captured during the Boer War.

Player: Was it Henry Stanley?

Leader: No. He lived during World War I.

Player: Was it Woodrow Wilson?

Leader: No. He lived during World War II.

Player: Was it Harry Truman?

Leader: No. He watched the London bombings during the Battle of Britain.

Player: Was it Winston Churchill?

Leader: Yes.

The winning player is now the new leader and a new game is ready to begin.

Relationships

■ Historic events are likely to be related to one another in a variety of ways. This game explores and reviews these relationships in world history. It can be played by three or more teams.

One team begins the game by naming two or three items from history. These items may be events, people, places, inventions, ideas, or any other thing important to history. After the pair or trio of things has been named, it is up to the other teams to determine the relationship which exists between or among the items listed.

The first player to correctly give a relationship scores a point for his team. He then gives the next set of events for the other teams to identify. It often happens that a perfectly good relationship will be cited which isn't the one the leader had in mind. In this case, award the team who gave the relationship a point but keep the game going until the relationship the leader had in mind is given. The player giving that relationship also receives a point and becomes the new leader. Should the group be unable to determine the relationship that the leader intended, the leader scores a point for his team and presents the group with another set of related items for identification.

The game looks like this in play.

Leader:	How are Joseph Stalin, Winston Churchill, and Franklin Roosevelt related?
First player:	They were all leaders.
Leader:	That is worth a point but it isn't my answer.
Second player:	They all lived during the Second World War.
Leader:	True and you get a point, but that wasn't my answer.
Third player:	They are all dead now.
Leader:	That's right for a point. What else?
Fourth player:	Their nations all fought Germany.
Leader:	Another point but still not my answer.

Play continues until, in this case, some student arrives at the idea that the three men all attended the Yalta Conference. In giving relationships, no points are awarded for such answers as "They were all men" or other obvious facts. If the names given had been those of Civil War generals, such an answer as "They are all dead now" would not be worthy of a point though it was given one in the previous illustration.

Relationships may be played again and again with good results.

Clever students will come up with some fascinating and off-beat relationships for consideration after they get the feel of the game.

Scrambles

■ Scrambles are just for fun. They can, and do, provide for a little review but are really more for fun than for specific learning.

A scramble is a word of historic or geographic significance which has been scrambled. Construction and use of scrambles is discussed fully on page 58.

There are several ways to use scrambles in the classroom for a few minutes' fun. One is for the teacher to prepare a list of scrambles to present to the entire class. Individuals may work at unscrambling these words, or students may pair off or work as small teams in an effort to be first to successfully unscramble the entire list.

Students enjoy making scrambles of their own. They enjoy exchanging lists of scrambles and holding contests.

Keep the contest under control by setting limits (categories, historic periods, etc.) to the scrambles used at any one time. For example, one set of scrambles might come from ancient Greece; another might deal with great generals from history.

A word of warning. Once you have challenged your class with a list of scrambles, expect a return challenge. Unless you have time on your hands, it may be well to turn down such a challenge. The kids are likely to give you a list which will keep you unscrambling into the early morning hours.

That's Life

■ Any number of games for history students seem to center around biographical information and identification. This is reasonable since many interesting facts are associated with the lives of the great. Here is yet another game dealing with biography, but with an interesting twist.

The leader opens the game by giving a fact about some person from history. If no one identifies the character, the leader gives another fact. Each time a fact is given and no one identifies the subject, he scores a point for himself. When any player is sure he knows the identity of the character, he gives a fact of his own. If the leader accepts this fact, the player scores a point for himself.

Now two people—the leader and one player—know the identity of the subject. Both continue giving facts alternately, scoring points for themselves. When another player discovers the identity, he also joins in giving facts. When three players have joined the leader, the round is over and the person to the right of the leader becomes the new leader for the next round. The game ends when everyone has had the same number of turns being leader.

This game is best played with smaller groups. Players keep their own scores, and at the end of play total their accumulated points for the session.

In the case of disputed questions, the leader will usually be able to identify a wrong statement at once. If there is no question in the leader's mind that a statement is wrong, he may say so at once. If there is a question, he says that the statement is questionable and at the end of play the question is resolved.

Players of any age can use this game, but with younger historians some adult supervision and possible refereeing is likely to be necessary from time to time.

In play the game goes in this fashion.

Leader:	He was English.
	He was once a news correspondent.
	He was First Lord of the Admiralty.
	He served in Parliament.
First player:	He was prime minister.
Leader:	He led England during World War II.
First player:	He was a Conservative.
Leader:	He went to many conferences as one of the Big Four.
First player:	He was called "Sir."
Second player:	He wrote many books.
Third player:	His first name is Winston.

Play ends here because there are now three players in on Churchill's identity. The leader scored 6 points, the first player scored 3, and the second and third players got a point each.

It doesn't take long before the leader and first successful player learn to keep their statements somewhat vague to allow them to amass as many points as possible.

That's Wrong!

■ Many of us delight in putting something over on our friends. Here is a game designed expressly for such students.

That's Wrong! calls for students to give facts concerning a given topic in oral rotation. A student may give a true or a false statement. There should be a brief pause before the next player begins speaking. During that second or two the other players must decide for themselves whether the statement just made was true or false. If a player feels the statement was true he keeps silent. If he thinks it is incorrect he calls out "That's wrong!" He then tells why it is wrong.

If the player calling "That's wrong!" is correct in his call, he receives a point and the player who was corrected loses a point. If, however, the player calling "That's wrong!" is incorrect in his thinking, he loses a point and the challenged player gains a point.

Should the player who gave an incorrect statement go unchallenged, he gains a point for himself as soon as the next player begins speaking.

In other words, the only way to gain points is to make shrewd but incorrect statements which aren't challenged, make true statements which sound false and are challenged, or to catch the false statement of another student.

The next student in turn gives a statement which may be either true or false, and so on around the group.

This game may use a given period in history, an event in history, the life of an historic character, etc. In play it goes like this. The subject here is Adolf Hitler. Statements are made in order (first, second, etc.), while challenges come from any other player.

First player:	He fought in World War I.
Second player:	Hitler was born in Prussia which helps explain his warlike attitude.
Another player:	That's wrong! He was born in Austria.

He gains a point and the second player loses one.

Third player:	Hitler became a corporal in World War I. War I.

Fourth player: He was in prison when he wrote his famous book, *Crusade in Europe*.

Fifth player: Hitler hated the Jews.

At this point the fourth player scored a point since he had given a false statement which was not caught by his fellow players.

Sixth player: Hitler and his wife Eva committed suicide when the Allies were closing in on Berlin.

Another player: That's wrong! Eva Braun wasn't his wife.

This player loses a point and player six gains one since Hitler married Eva before their death.

Seventh player: Some of Hitler's own men tried to kill him with a bomb.

And so it goes. A good variation of this game requires a student to present a short report of two or three paragraphs on a person or event. In the report, he gives one incorrect fact or draws a faulty conclusion. The listeners attempt to find his error. Those who catch the error score a point while those who don't lose a point. Anyone who challenges a correct statement loses 2 points for his error.

They Are Related

■ Only the quick-witted will survive for long in this game. The opening player names a person, place, or event from history. He turns to the next player and counts to ten at a moderate rate. Before he reaches ten, the player he indicates must name a person, place, or event which is related in some way to the item given.

As soon as the player gives a related item, he turns to another player and begins counting. That player must supply a related item. He, in turn, indicates another player as play progresses around the group.

Any player who can't supply a related answer loses a point. Any player whose answer is challenged must explain his answer. If he can't, he loses a point. If he can prove a relationship, he scores a point and the challenger loses one.

No item once used may be reused in the course of a game.

A good variation is for a student to call on the next player by name instead of going around the room in order. This random choice keeps every player on his toes and makes for a far more exciting game. Using this variation, the game is played as follows.

Opening player:	George Washington. Joe. (*starts counting*)
Joe:	Martha. Jill. (*starts counting*)
Jill:	Mount Vernon. Larry. (*starts counting*)
Larry:	Potomac River. Bruce. (*starts counting*)
Bruce:	Washington, D.C. Jill. (*starts counting*)
Jill:	White House. Janice. (*starts counting*)

And the game goes on.

What Came Next?

■ Chronology is important to the understanding of history. This game provides an excellent review of historic chronology and is fun at the same time. It is an easily explained game that requires a lot of thought and challenges the players.

The beginning player gives an event from history or a happening in the life of a noted character from history. He then asks the next player. "What came next?" It is the job of the player so asked to supply an event or happening which followed the event just cited. He, in turn, asks the next player to tell "What came next?" and play goes around the group.

Any player unable to supply a fact or who gives an out-of-sequence fact loses a point. Successful players score a point for each correct answer. The game's object is to keep play going as long as possible by giving events which happened fairly close to one another. When a topic has been exhausted, another topic may be chosen and play continues. When general historic events are used, only one long game is usually played at a sitting. It is often best to limit the span of a game when general history is used. The period of American colonization or the history of Greece and Rome would make for fairly good games which wouldn't last overly long.

If the American Revolution were used, the game might progress like this.

First player:	Taxes were needed to pay the cost of the French and Indian War. What came next?

Second player:	The Proclamation of 1763 was issued. What came next?
Third player:	The Stamp Act was passed. What came next?
Fourth player:	The Sons of Liberty were organized. What came next?
Fifth player:	The Boston Massacre occurred. What came next?
Sixth player:	The Boston Tea Party angered the British. What came next?
Seventh player:	The First Continental Congress met. What came next?
Eighth player:	The Intolerable Acts were passed.

This player loses a point since his fact came before the First Continental Congress.

And on and on. It might be well to note this game is a bit hard. For less able students it can be used successfully as an open-book review. Though the open book may sound too easy, it isn't. A fast-moving game with books open requires a lot more skill than one might assume. Try it and see.

Where Are You From?

■ Play begins with one student acting as leader. He picks a place with historic significance, writes his choice on a slip of paper, then gives the other players clues to its location. After each clue, the players may attempt to guess the location in question. When the players feel they need more information, one asks, "Where are you from?" The leader must then supply an additional clue.

It is obvious that the leader will want to begin with rather vague clues in order to preserve his turn as leader longer. He must, however, supply an additional clue each time he is asked, "Where are you from?" When a student finally discovers the identity of the historic place, that student becomes the new leader.

The game might go something like this.

Leader:	I lived fairly close to the sea.
Player:	Are you from England?
Leader:	No.

Player:	Are you from Egypt?
Leader:	No.
Player:	Where are you from?
Leader:	I'm from a place which was famous long ago.
Player:	Are you from China?
Leader:	No.
Player:	Are you from Japan?
Leader:	No.
Player:	Where are you from?
Leader:	I am from a place where many brave men lived.
Player:	Do you live on an island?
Leader:	No.

And so on until Sparta is guessed and a new round begins.

Where in the World?

■ This is a quiz-type game. The question, "Where in the world might you see _____ ?" includes the name of something from history. The players then attempt to guess the place the leader has in mind. After three unsuccessful guesses, the leader repeats the question, "Where is the world might you see _____ ?" and adds another item to the one he previously gave. Three more attempts to guess the location of the place follow. If all are unsuccessful the question, "Where in the world might you see _____ "? is expanded, giving three things to be seen. This procedure continues, with the leader adding one item after every three unsuccessful guesses until some astute player is able to locate the place the leader had in mind.

The game proceeds in this fashion.

Leader:	Where in the world might you see a great naval battle?
Player:	Was it in the English Channel?
Leader:	No.
Player:	Was it in the Mediterranean Sea?
Leader:	No.
Player:	Was it in the Atlantic Ocean?

Leader:	No. Where in the world might you see a great naval battle in which a Spanish fleet was defeated?
Player:	Was it in the Caribbean Sea?
Leader:	No.
Player:	Was it near Spain?
Leader:	No.

The guessing and additional information continue until, in this case, the Battle of Manila Bay is identified and a new game begins.

Who Was _____ When?

■ Here is an ideal team game for small groups who have a bit of time in which to work as a team in putting the game together. Once the game is ready to go, the teams challenge one another. Who Was _____ When? consists of a series of five events which happened during the life of an individual—the reign or rule of a king, president, dictator, etc.

One team begins play by asking "Who was_____when?" and then reading the first event on the list. The other player or team is then allowed one guess at the ruler or other individual in question. If that guess is correct, the successful team scores 5 points. If it is incorrect, a second event is read. Another guess is then allowed, but this guess if correct is worth only 4 points. Events and guesses alternate until the guessing team is successful or until the fifth incorrect guess is made. If the final event does not lead the guessing team to the answer, then the team posing the problem scores 10 points.

As soon as one set of events has been used, the game alternates with the other team or player presenting events and the guesses coming from the starting team. This continues until time runs out or a predetermined score is reached.

The game goes like this.

Team I:	Who was president of the United States when the first oil well was drilled?
Team II:	Grover Cleveland?
Team I:	Wrong. Who was president when the Pony Express was started?

Team II: Abraham Lincoln?
Team I: Wrong. Who was president when John Brown attacked Harper's Ferry?
Team II: James Buchanan.
Team I: Correct.

Team II scores 3 points for the answer and becomes the new questioner.

Team II: Who was king of England when the War of the Spanish Succession was fought?

And the game is again underway.

■ PUZZLE-QUIZZES

Puzzle-quizzes come in a variety of shapes and sizes and are popular with students of almost any age. The educationally reluctant as well as the educationally advanced take delight in solving the puzzle-quiz. It is a matter of adapting a given puzzle-quiz to the ability and interest levels of students.

Puzzle-quizzes are ideal for use in introducing a new area of study, as study guides to direct student reading, for review of a unit of work, or even as a testing device. The ideas which follow will assist you in preparing puzzle-quizzes.

Constructing their own puzzle-quizzes offers a wide range of learning experiences to students. Student-constructed puzzle-quizzes are quite popular and can be used as excellent unit review and study devices. The teacher should set the ground rules as to puzzle type, extent of material to be covered, and time in which to build the puzzle. The rest is up to the students. It is always a good idea for each student to keep a note of the correct answer and page source for each item in a puzzle-quiz. Not only is this a good study habit but it can also head off many an argument at the pass.

The completed projects may be exchanged among students for additional study and review.

Biographical Puzzlers

■ Identification of biographical sketches and items related to important historical characters is an interesting puzzle-quiz. The four types of biographical puzzlers which follow illustrate possible variations that may be used.

> I was born in England in 1600. Twenty-five years later I was crowned king. I believed strongly in the Divine Right of kings. During the first four years of my rule, I called Parliament into session three times but dissolved each session because the members didn't act as I wished. From 1629 until 1640 I ruled without Parliament. When I needed money to fight Scottish rebels, I called another Parliament in 1640. A few weeks later the famous Long Parliament was called which stayed in session until after my death. I tried to imprison some leaders of Parliament in 1642 and a civil war broke out. In 1645 I fled to Scotland to escape Cromwell's armies, but the Scots returned me to England. In 1649 I was convicted of treason and beheaded. Who was I? (Charles I)

The biographical sketch of Charles I covers the high points of the life of a ruler, and it also has a much broader scope because it covers the high points of an important period in history.

The biographical puzzle-sketch which follows is a "slice of life" biography, in that it deals with one event in the life of an historic person.

> It was a grim day in 1536 for the woman. In a few hours she was to be beheaded. She was not quite thirty. Her husband had tired of her and was having her executed for a crime she insisted she had not committed. He claimed she was unfaithful to him. Her husband was the most powerful man in the land, and he was to have his way. Only a few years before, her husband had tired of his first wife. He had divorced her to marry the woman now waiting to die. Though no one knew it in 1536, the daughter of the condemned

woman would one day rule the nation. The faithless husband would acquire four more wives during his lifetime.

Who was the woman about to lose her head?
Anne Boleyn
Mary, Queen of Scots
Elizabeth the Great   (Anne Boleyn)

Who was the husband who thought so little of his wives?
Charles I
Henry VIII
Richard I   (Henry VIII)

The biographical puzzler which follows is actually more of a quiz. Four or five (or more) events in the life of an individual are given. They need not appear in chronological order—for more able groups, scrambled order would make it more challenging. Students are to identify the person from the clues given. This activity is a variation of Lives of the Great from the chapter on Games in this book.

What South American . . .
1. Took a trip to the United States in 1807 and got some ideas concerning free government?
2. Began to fight for Latin American independence in 1810?
3. Was called the Liberator?
4. Was elected president of Venezuela in 1819?
5. Was also president of Columbia in 1819?
                                       (Simón Bolívar)

You can score this quiz by assigning points to the questions. If the student supplies the correct answer after the first clue, he receives 5 points for his team. Four points are awarded for an answer on the second clue, and so on in descending order.

This final example of a biographical quiz is not so strong on biography as it is on the puzzle aspect. It involves bits of biographical information as well as clues to the spelling of the name. The example shows how.

_ _ _ _ _ _ _ _

o o o   x x x

1. He encouraged his soldiers to marry women in countries the army conquered.

2. The letters marked *x* spell a conjunction.
3. The letters marked *o* name a beverage.
4. Though he died at the age of thirty-three, his name is remembered as The Great, for he conquered most of the then known world during his short lifetime.

(Alexander)

As a teacher-prepared lesson, biographical puzzlers are fine. As a student project in creative writing and historic research, they are outstanding.

Codes

■ Since man began writing, he has had reason to keep some of his messages secret from prying eyes.

Codes are limited only by the imagination of the code maker. There is no correct or incorrect way to make a code, though a few rules are in order for the uninitiated. Code-making and code-breaking must follow a few rules. In general, code-breaking depends upon the location and identification of the vowels. Watch for single letters which must be the words *a* or *I* in messages. Then work into two- and three-letter words which must, of course, contain a vowel.

In the history classroom, coded quotations of historic value are good items for encoding and decoding. It is often desirable to give some clue about the content of the quotation, or even to fill in a starting letter to get students going.

This is definitely an activity for your above average and average students, though slow learners can handle simple decoding with clues and individual help.

It is only a short step from breaking codes to making codes. Code-making is an excellent student activity, though a word of caution might be in order. Don't volunteer to decode one student's puzzle unless you are ready to accept all challenges. Unless you're a code expert with time on your hands, you'll run the risks of being inundated with coded messages or of hurting the feelings of those whose challenges you must turn aside. When you are elbow deep in unbreakable codes, just remember—we warned you.

This first example is a simple code in which one letter is substituted for another in alphabetical order. As soon as one letter is established, the rest fall into line easily.

> J FTUBCMJTIFE MBX BOE KVTUJDF JO UIF MBOE.   JBNNVSBCJ
> I established law and justice in the land.   Hammurabi

Note that the entire coded quotation is shown in capitals. Also note that the source is given. A quotation without its source is only half a quotation.

The following coded quotation might be introduced as a translation from a noted Greek poet who lived some twenty-seven hundred years ago. With this clue, the poet's name should be easily decoded, and the quotation is simple to decode from that point. Again, this is a patterned code and easy to solve after a letter or two is established.

> QM CLBQ RFC ZJMMBW ZSQGLCQQ MD RFC BYW.   FMKCP
> So ends the bloody business of the day.   Homer

If the students don't decode Homer on the basis of the "Greek poet" clue, give them a start by saying *C* in the code stands for *e* in the quotation.

Remember when constructing coded quotations to beware of extremely short quotations unless there is some easy clue. Longer quotations give the student a fighting chance to find repeated letters. Without *a*'s, *i*'s or an easily decoded author, the short quotation can be impossible unless a letter is given as a starter.

Here is an example of a short quotation which is easily broken once the class is told it is an English translation of words spoken by a Roman general turned statesman.

> T HDWA, T ODX, T HCVGLABAR.   ZDTLO KLETLO HDAODB
> I came, I saw, I conquered.   Gaius Julius Caesar

From time to time it is fair to throw in a letter which represents itself. Never, however, use a code letter to represent more than one letter. (For example, *T* could not be used for both *m* and *h*.) Impress the importance of this rule on student code builders.

Any time a group gets stuck on a coded quotation, give them a letter as a starter.

Though codes shouldn't occupy any great portion of history time, they are interesting and often lead to out-of-class activity. With this in mind, a copy of *Bartlett's Familiar Quotations* is a must for the social studies classroom.

In closing, we leave the following code which has a message for all teachers and students of history. *A* in the code is *t* in the original quotation.

ABC DEFJ ABGEH IC BKLC AD MCKN GO MCKN GAOCFM.

MNKEPFGE QCFKED NDDOCLCFA

Criss-Crosses

■ The criss-cross is one of the best puzzle-quizzes for the social studies class. The criss-cross can be adapted to students of any ability or grade level. It is unlike a conventional crossword puzzle in that every word used relates to the puzzle topic. There is no need for extraneous words to connect the puzzle parts.

The first step in constructing a criss-cross is to collect the words to be included in the puzzle. Write these in an alphabetical list. Use quarter-inch squared paper or draw the grid lines on plain paper. Lay out the puzzle by placing the words in the grid in criss-cross fashion.

Begin in the upper left-hand corner and work down and to the right. Whenever possible, interlock your words more than once. Try to keep the puzzle as compact as possible, though this becomes increasingly difficult when numerous lengthy words are used. Avoid blank spaces of only one square. Every empty space should contain at least two squares, if possible.

When the puzzle is completed, number the beginning square of each word. Number from left to right, line by line. Be sure each beginning letter receives a number. Now construct your clues. You will have two sets—across and down.

For younger or less able students, it is sometimes desirable to list words below the puzzle from which to choose answers. Such a list may contain only the words needed for the puzzle, or additional related words may be included as foils. For older or more able classes, such a list of words is unnecessary.

The best uses of these puzzles are to introduce a new unit of work or to review. In such cases it is a good idea to follow each clue with the page number on which the answer may be found. This allows students to find the desired answers without needless hunting and fumbling.

When the completed puzzle has been checked and double checked, transfer it to a duplicator master for student use. Clip or tape the puzzle to a duplicator master, and use a ruler and a firm hand in tracing the puzzle outline. You can also use the Thermofax to make a master from the puzzle outline. Remember to trace *only* those squares the students will need to write letters in. Be sure to do the tracing on a firm surface.

As with any student project, make sure your instructions are clear and your puzzle correct before giving it to the students. After you have tried the criss-cross, you will never be without it. For class work, for fast finishers, for slow learners, or as extra work for fun, it has no equal. What's more, the kids love it. The extra work involved in construction is more than adequately repaid by student interest and enthusiasm.

Here are the directions and clues for the sample criss-cross in Figure 6.

Directions: Follow the clues below to complete the puzzle. Each set of squares can be filled correctly with only one word or phrase. Be sure the answers you choose completely fill the squares in the puzzle. Also, be sure each time an answer crosses another that the letters match where the two words cross.

ACROSS

 1. During the industrial revolution, the use of _____ enabled one worker to produce great amounts of goods daily.
 4. Money used to pay for factories is called _____.
 7. A large building used to house many workers and machines.
 9. The _____ engine provided the power needed to turn hundreds of machines in great factories.
 10. Karl _____ felt factory workers were not receiving a fair share of what they produced. His ideas included violent revolution in which workers gained control of the government.
 11. Another name for workers.
 12. Money made by businessmen is called _____.

13. Workers' pay.
15. Name of system which has no government control and regulation of business.
17. A nation which tries to sell goods to another nation's customers is a _____.
18. Before the industrial revolution, most goods were produced by _____ _____.
19. The steam engine was used for transportation when the railroad _____ was built.

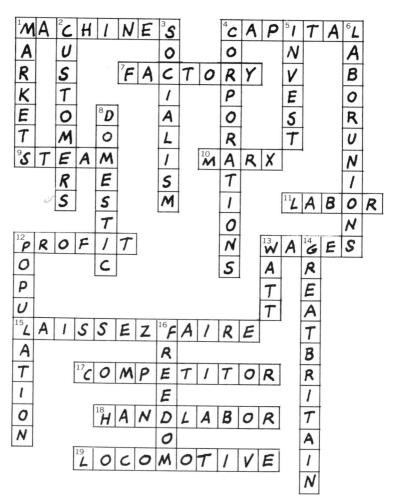

Figure 6. A sample criss-cross on the industrial revolution.

Down

1. Places where goods are sold.
2. People who buy manufactured goods.
3. A form of government in which many large industries are controlled by the national government.
4. Companies formed for the purpose of investing the money of many individuals.
5. To spend money to build factories is to _____ it.
6. When working conditions became too terrible during the industrial revolution, workers formed _____ _____ in order to attempt to improve things.
8. When goods were produced by hand labor in the homes of workers, it was known as the _____ system.
12. As better farming methods and better medicine allowed more people to be fed and to live longer, the number of people increased. This caused a growth in the _____ of industrial nations.
13. James _____ improved the steam engine until it could be used to provide power for factories.
14. In what nation did the industrial revolution begin? (*two words*)
16. The system of wage bargaining in which each worker bargained for his own wages was called _____ of contract.

The sample puzzle in Figure 6 was intended for use as a quick review of the industrial revolution. Had it been an introductory puzzle, the page numbers on which the answers could be found would have followed each question or clue. Remember, a list of the twenty-three answers plus a few extra foils might well follow the puzzle for classes of less able students.

As a review activity, student-constructed criss-crosses are particularly effective.

Letter Mazes

■ A letter maze consists of a number of correctly spelled, related words. These words are already written in the maze horizontally, vertically, or diagonally. They are spelled both forwards and backwards. Words overlap one another throughout the maze.

In constructing such a maze, begin at the upper left-hand corner and work to the right and down filling in words as you go on a piece of graph paper. Whenever possible, overlap the letters of one word with those of another. Keep your maze in the general shape of a rectangle. Don't allow long words to protrude any distance from the remainder of the maze.

Once the maze has been constructed, fill in empty spaces with random letters until your maze forms a perfect rectangle. For quick checking, you might use a different colored pencil for these random letters on your master or working copy.

```
U  N  I  T  E  D  S  T  A  T  E  S

P  O  R  I  N  I  L  O  S  S  U  M

O  S  E  I  L  L  A  -  -  A  G  -

L  L  L  N  A  P  A  J  X  -  A  -

A  I  T  A  I  P  O  I  H  T  E  -

N  W  I  -  -  -  S  I  T  A  L  Y

D  -  H  G  E  R  M  A  N  Y  -  -
```

Figure 7. A clued letter maze—without random letters.

It is a simple matter to transfer the completed maze from the original copy with a typewriter, as has been done in Figure 7. It is also a simple matter to place your maze on a duplicator master by clipping or taping your original copy to the duplicator working surface and tracing the letters with a firm hand, or to make a Thermofax duplicator master.

The two basic maze types are those with clues and those without. Examples of both types follow. In both types, related words are used to build the maze. With either type of maze, be sure the students understand the directions in which words in the maze may be written. Students should circle words as they find them in a maze. Keep in mind that diagonally written words are the most difficult to locate in a maze. Diagonal words spelled backwards are the hardest of all and are best avoided with slower or younger students. In some cases, it may be advisable to construct mazes with only horizontal and vertical words in left-right and top-bottom order (no reversals).

The maze in Figure 7 contains only a dozen answers. The students answer the fill-in questions below the maze before locating the hidden answers in the maze. In order to better show construction details, this maze is incomplete. The random letters have not been filled in. If this maze were to be used in class, all blank spaces would contain random letters to square off the maze. Of course, complete instructions to the class would precede the maze.

CLUES

1. Following World War I, a world-wide peace-keeping organization was set up. It was called the _____ of Nations. (League)
2. This organization had been the idea of United States President, Woodrow _____. (Wilson)
3. A major Western nation failed to join this organization. That nation was the _____ _____. (United States)
4. In the 1930's, the world could see peace was not being kept. In 1931, _____ attacked Manchuria. (Japan)
5. Four years later, Italy invaded the African nation of _____. The international peace-keeping organization was unable to stop either the Japanese or the Italians. (Ethiopia)
6. Germany's leader, Adolph _____, was encouraged by the success of the Italians, ruled by Benito _____. The two nations signed an allegiance in 1936 and became the _____ Powers. (Hitler, Mussolini, Axis)
7. Two years later, _____ invaded its neighbor, Czechoslovakia and the next year Albania fell to _____. (Germany, Italy)
8. On September 1, 1939, Germany invaded _____. Two days later, World War II officially began when Great Britain and France declared war on Germany. The nations opposing Germany were known as the _____. (Poland, Allies)

Note that the clues in the letter maze in Figure 7 are actually little more than a conventional study guide for World War II.

The maze adds to student enjoyment and serves to reinforce the facts mentioned in the guide. It is this reinforcement idea which makes the maze valuable.

Figure 8 shows another example of the clued maze that can be quite useful. In this case, a maze is constructed with all answers either horizontal or vertical. Some words will read from right to left or bottom to top. Each question refers to a horizontal row or vertical column in the maze. In this way, the student can answer the question by locating the correct word.

The partial maze in Figure 8, with no random letters filled in, illustrates the point.

```
        a  b  c  d  e  f  g  h  i  j

   1  |  G  E  R  M  A  N  Y  —  —  A
   2  |  —  —  —  U  —  —  —  —  —  X
   3  |  —  —  —  N  A  P  A  J  —  I
   4  |  —  —  E  I  S  S  A  L  E  S
   5  |  —  —  —  C  —  —  —  —  —  —
   6  |  —  —  —  H  —  —  —  —  —  —
```

Figure 8. Another clued letter maze. When completed, random letters would take the place of the dashes.

CLUES

  1. Germany and Italy were members of the _____ Powers during World War II. (Column j)
  2. Russia and _____ signed a treaty on August 23, 1939. (Row 1)
  3. _____ invaded Manchuria in 1936. (Row 3)
  4. Haile _____ was emperor of Ethiopia when Italy attacked that nation. (Row 4)
  5. At the _____ Conference in September, 1938, Hitler was given the Sudetenland for Germany. (Column d)

And on through the puzzle.

The large maze in Figure 9 is completed, with random letters in place. It is a search-and-find maze with no clues save the one given in the title. Of course, the instructions to the students would again mention what the students are seeking and would explain

```
Y U G O S L A V I A I L A R T S U A A E M
E N E T H E R L A N D S A B R A Z I L T F
K I N B E L G I U M H O N D U R A S A H L
R T I Y B V E N R Q N E L I H C I O M I Q
U E A A C A N A D A O E D A E O B V E O U
T D R U Z W T H D R N C E I L S M I T P G
U K K G E A I D N I A N N V S T O E A I D
N I U U C A N U M B B A M I A A L T U A N
I N Z R H G A R I Y E R A L L R O U G O A
T G R U O B M E X U L F R O V I C N A U L
E D E K S H T P Y G E D K B A C T I R Y A
D O E O L G R E E C E N S J D A Q O A A E
S M C C O L I B E R I A O R O F H N C U Z
T N U I V E N E Z U E L A V R E A C I G W
A T A X A M A N A P N O R W A Y I P N A E
T L D E K P H I L I P P I N E S T X J R N
E D O M I N I C A N R E P U B L I C D A I
S Y R I A C I R F A H T U O S S K C R P P
W H I T E R U S S I A I B A R A I D U A S
```

Argentina	Ethiopia	Panama
Australia	France	Paraguay
Belgium	Greece	Peru
Bolivia	Guatemala	Philippines
Brazil	Haiti	Poland
Canada	Honduras	Saudi Arabia
Chile	India	South Africa
China	Iran	Soviet Union
Colombia	Iraq	Syria
Costa Rica	Lebanon	Turkey
Cuba	Liberia	Ukraine
Czechoslovakia	Luxembourg	United Kingdom
Denmark	Mexico	United States
Dominican Republic	Netherlands	Uruguay
Ecuador	New Zealand	Venezuela
Egypt	Nicaragua	White Russia
El Salvador	Norway	Yugoslavia

Figure 9. Fifty-one original members of the United Nations.

how the maze works. Obviously, this type of maze is appropriate for older, advanced groups, since it is virtually clueless and uses diagonals and reversals. It may be desirable to give the students a list of the words to be located in the maze, as shown with the example of the United Nations maze.

Letter Mixtures

■ Letter mixtures require mixing the letters from several answers into one alphabetical list. This mixture is followed by several questions or clues which lead the student to the desired answer. In a letter mixture the student uses each letter given in spelling the answers needed to the questions. When the correct answers have been spelled, all letters in the mixture will have been used and none will be left over.

The following examples show how letter mixtures work.

a a c e e e g i k l n n r r s s s s t t u

1. Name of the people from the north who settled Rome about 750 B.C. (Latins)
2. People from Asia Minor who settled western Italy and ruled Rome until about 500 B.C. (Etruscans)
3. People who taught the Latins the alphabet and religion. (Greeks)

A harder variation of the letter mixture puzzle-quiz gives the student a general clue and the letter mixture.

a a a a a a a a c c c
d e e e e g g g h
i i i i l m m n n n
o o p r r r s s t u

In this letter mixture are the names of six areas conquered and ruled by the Romans. Find them. (Carthage, Macedonia, Spain, Greece, Asia Minor, Gaul)

As an additional clue, you could capitalize those letters that begin each word. In the first example, you would have three capitals—an *L*, an *E*, and a *G*; in the second, there would be seven capitals—*C*, *M*, *S*, *A*, *M*, and two *G*'s.

Places in History

■ This puzzle-quiz works as well as a contest as it does as a puzzle. Four or five facts about a place of historic or geographic significance are presented and from these factual clues students determine the place in question. This place may be a city, a nation, a battle site, or perhaps a building.

This is another quiz which can be used as a contest by assigning points in reverse value to the clues. In other words, give a student 5 points for correctly identifying the place in question on the first clue. The second clue is worth only 4 points, and so on in descending order.

Here is how the clues might be set up.

1. This structure was built over two thousand years ago.
2. It was to protect the nation's people from invasion.
3. Workers who died on the project were often thrown into the structure to become part of it.
4. It is about fifteen hundred miles long and twenty-five feet high.
5. This structure is in the most populated country of the world.

(Great Wall of China)

1. This famous battle was fought in June, 1815.
2. It ended the power of a European emperor.
3. The battle site was in Belgium.
4. Wellington commanded the English forces.
5. Napoleon led the unsuccessful French in this battle.

(The Battle of Waterloo)

Again, don't overlook the value and fun in having students construct their own games.

Scrambled Letters

■ The scrambled letter puzzle-quiz is one of the easiest to construct. It can be relatively easy or quite difficult to solve, depending upon its construction. This particular puzzle-quiz is best suited to elementary and junior high students. It is an especially popular type of construction for the students to make themselves.

The following examples illustrate several forms of the scrambled-letter puzzle. As can be seen, the beginning letter of each scramble is the beginning letter of the correctly spelled word.

> 1. The Sumerians lived along two river valleys. What were the two rivers named? *Tisgri, Eratupehs (Tigris,* Euphrates)
> 2. The Sumerians eventually joined a number of cities into one nation. What was this land called? *Matopseoima* (Mesopotamia)

A slightly harder puzzle follows. Note that no capitals are used and the first letter of the scramble is not the first letter of the intended answer.

> 1. When a city had its own government, it became what was really a small nation. What name is given to such cities? *ticy-tasset* (city-states)
> 2. The Sumerians developed a way of storing water and moving water from rivers to thirsty crops. What is this called? *gatnoriiri* (irrigation)

In somewhat more difficult form of the game, provide a list of scrambled words related to a given area of study. The students then unscramble the words in the list. As an extension, you may wish to have students use the unscrambled words in sentences or in a short report on the unit. The following scrambles might be used when Sumer is being studied.

gritis virre (Tigris River)	*mersunsia* (Sumerians)
labbyno (Babylon)	*funcermio* (cuneiform)
salw (laws)	*labtets* (tablets)
girtirnaio (irrigation)	*gurgiztas* (ziggurats)

A slightly fancier approach involves constructing scrambles in the form of anagrams. They might look like this.

1. Wedge-shaped writing   *I comer fun* (cuneiform)
2. High temples   *rut gas zig* (ziggurats)

Triples

■ A triple (or quadruple, or more if desired) is an effective study puzzle-quiz with a number of possible uses. Primarily, triples are used to indicate relationships. They may be adapted to almost any phase of history. The two sets of examples which follow show the basic sets of triples.

Each of the items in a group is related to the others. Tell how the items are related.

1. Christopher Columbus
   Cabeza de Vaca
   Fernando de Soto
   (explored for Spain)

2. Father Jacques Marquette and Louis Joliet
   Sieur de La Salle
   Fernando de Soto
   (explored the Mississippi River)

In each of the following groups of names, one does not belong. Which item is out of place in each group? Why?

1. Aztecs, Incas, Vikings   (Vikings aren't Indians)
2. Henry Hudson, John Cabot, Leif Ericson
   (Ericson wasn't an English explorer)
3. Hernando Cortez, Francisco Pizarro, Amerigo Vespucci
   (Vespucci didn't conquer Indian nations)
4. Ferdinand Magellan, Francisco Coronado, Sir Francis
   Drake   (Coronado didn't sail around the world)

When using triples, be on the alert for answers which are correct but not what you had in mind. Quite often items are related in more than one way. Also, it is entirely possible for an item to be unrelated to others in a way other than the one you selected. Too, a different item than the one you chose may be unrelated for a good reason.

▪ WRITING PROJECTS

In this unit you will find a number of activities that will encourage students to write independently and creatively. These activities can be scaled up or down in difficulty to meet student needs and abilities.

In some instances there is likely to be some overlapping of themes here and elsewhere in the book.

Diaries

▪ Since man began writing, he has kept a record of his comings and goings. Among the most important records in history have been diaries of people involved in history-making events.

Diaries of the greats from history have given modern researchers invaluable material concerning given periods in the history of the world. The political, economic, and social conditions of a time are reflected in these diaries. Powerful people—kings, governors, and military leaders—have kept diaries. Artists and writers have contributed to our knowledge of a period of time from their remarks concerning the mores, dress, and education of the day.

Even more revealing at times have been the diaries kept by private individuals. These often give an entirely different picture of the period. They reflect the conditions of individuals who had no control over the affairs of state but who were controlled by those same affairs.

Diaries not intended for publication are often the best in terms of historic interest. The diary kept by Samuel Pepys is a good example.

Enough about historic people and their diaries, however. The diaries of history students are those which interest us at the moment. Assigning students to write historic diaries gives free rein to their creative urges while requiring them to make rather careful research. A student assumes the identity of a character long dead and prepares his diary as it might have been written.

Such a diary can be as long or as short as the student wishes to make it. A day in the life of an historic character might cover one page. The same character might be taken through an entire year. Obviously, such an assignment must be geared to student abilities and interests.

There are thousands of possible diary assignments. Here are some ideas to set you thinking and illustrate the endless possibilities in diary writing.

A day in the life of a boy of Sumer
A week's entries of an overseer in the building of the Great Pyramid
A soldier with Hannibal from Carthage to Rome
A day with a Roman senator
A day at a Roman circus
The highlights of a year in the life of a page during the Middle Ages
A knight's account of a Crusade
Martin Luther's life about the beginning of the Reformation
The secret diary of a sailor with Columbus
A soldier with Cortez in Mexico
A year in the life of a Jamestown settler
A soldier's months at Valley Forge with Washington
An account of a journey from Missouri to Oregon by covered wagon
A Confederate soldier's account of the Battle of Gettysburg
John Wilkes Booth's diary during the days immediately before Lincoln's assassination
A doughboy's life in a trench in France in 1917

A Kansas farmer's thoughts during the Depression years of 1931 and 1932

The diary of a British shopkeeper during the Battle of Britain

Letter Writing

■ The writing of letters from history is one of the many assignments which allow students some creative thinking combined with historic learning. They may write letters from the viewpoint of any historic individual desired. The letter writer may be a great leader or an imaginary commoner. Likewise, the recipient of the letter may be an actual historic character or an imaginary individual.

The one thing that must remain constant in this project, however, is that the letter's content must be in keeping with the period in which the writer lived. No matter how much creative thought goes into such a letter, the content must be well researched and accurate.

Possible letter writing projects might involve the following people.

A soldier with Alexander writing to his wife

A Spartan boy to his girl friend

A Roman tribune to a senator concerning upcoming legislation

A nobleman to a knight concerning a coming conflict

A boy applying to a guild member for apprenticeship in the guild

A general in Napoleon's army writing to his son before the beginning of the Russian invasion

A Confederate youth writing to his Northern uncle shortly before the battle at Bull Run

President Wilson writing the German ambassador concerning Germany's unrestricted submarine warfare

An Oklahoma farmer writing to his brother as he prepared to move his family to California in search of work in 1933

A Russian at Stalingrad writing to his brother in Moscow following the seige at Stalingrad

Winston Churchill writing to President Roosevelt concerning the possibility of a meeting with Stalin

A survivor of the atomic attack at Hiroshima writing to a friend in Tokyo

An Israeli pilot writing to his wife following the first day of the Six-Day War

News Releases

■ Writing news releases covering historic events is an interesting activity which allows considerable leeway for the creative student while requiring research and attention to detail.

Stress that all good reporting is concerned with answering five questions: Who? What? When? Where? and Why? A sixth question which may or may not have bearing on the article is How? With these questions in mind, the student has a head start on planning any news article. If these questions are answered by the article, it is likely to be a good piece of research.

News releases may be assigned to a class or to individuals. However, it is seldom a good idea—and a considerable waste of student energies—to assign the same news article to all members of a class. Such an assignment jams the resources and puts maximum effort into minimum coverage. A reasonable class assignment might call for a number of related articles.

Collecting a number of articles from the same general historic period into a newspaper is a possible class project. When assigning historic news releases, keep in mind that such an assignment should be specific and narrow in scope. A limited topic can be covered in a fairly brief time, giving the student a feeling of accomplishment.

Some topics suited to news release writing are given here. Remember that some research should be required in writing such a release. The amount of necessary research can be adjusted to meet student ability.

Brown's raid at Harper's Ferry
One of Stuart's rides circling the Union troops
The capture of John Wilkes Booth
The sinking of the *Lusitania*
The signing of the Armistice ending World War I
The Beer Hall Putsh
The Reichstag fire

The Pearl Harbor attack
MacArthur's return to the Philippines
The death of Benito Mussolini
A Ghandi hunger strike
The invasion of South Korea
The Tonkin Bay incident

Quiz Questions

■ Student-prepared quizzes are extremely effective study and review exercises. Additionally, this activity is highly motivational and challenging for the students.

In preparing quiz questions, the students should be limited to the material dealing with a given unit of study or period in history. Their sources should also be limited to those read (or supposedly read) by all class members. Within these limits, almost anything goes.

Encourage students to prepare a variety of questions including multiple choice, true/false, matching, completion, and other short-answer types. Students should also include the correct answers and the sources for their questions—in case they are challenged to supply the answers. This last point is of utmost importance. There is nothing more frustrating for a student than having an excellent question challenged and then being unable to refute the challenge.

Questions prepared by students may be used in a variety of ways. For example, an excellent class review could be based on the student questions written in connection with the games discussed earlier in this book. The review could take the form of the original game, a contest, or simply an oral exercise. Another good use of student questions is in a graded quiz or test. There is no reason not to use student questions, provided they have been checked for accuracy and have been evaluated to avoid poor or duplicate questions.

Encourage the students to do the best possible job of question writing by selecting the best questions for use in the game, quiz, or test. Since the students supplying these questions will already know the correct answers, they will have a definite advantage over their classmates—an added incentive for doing their best in writing questions.

Most students appreciate the challenge about the affair and find it fun to outwit their neighbors with really good quiz questions. Of course, this can lead to excesses from time to time. When a student quiz maker asks, "How many Indians are in the picture on page 146?" there is some question about the validity and relevance of that particular question. It can't be used on a graded test, of course. However, such a question tossed in from time to time in a game, contest, or other activity isn't all that bad. It may bring a few groans amid the laughs and the inability to answer may be just the thing for the opposite team in a contest. This is especially true when the question was supplied by the little guy in the corner who never gets any recognition because he never does anything well—and when his victim is the class brain. When this happens, allow the question and give the little guy credit for it. However, for obvious reasons, such questions should not be continuously encouraged.

Try answering your students' questions before looking at their answers. The results may surprise you and give you a bit more sympathy for the kids when they take your next test.

▪ PHYSICAL ACTIVITIES

The word *physical* here doesn't imply great amounts of dashing about. However, the activities in this chapter do require more than reading and writing. The written aspect of history is not left out of these activities, nor is research which is needed for any study of history. Instead, these activities require some art and offer the student the opportunity to learn by means other than straight reading and writing.

In this area we present activities that give social studies students a change of pace and allow for creativity. Some of these ideas are suited to the student who finds reading and writing a chore—if not an impossibility. A reluctant student may take an interest in some of these projects, gain success and recognition from his peers, and decide that history isn't so bad after all!

Though it may be unnecessary, we'll include a note of caution. *Some* slow students have artistic talent, but this is the exception, not the rule. The bright student is also likely to be the creative student.

AV Corners

▪ A few years ago, most teachers never considered allowing students to operate audiovisual equipment. More recently, open concept teaching that encourages students to use this equipment as learning materials is common in many classrooms today. Cassette recorders, low-wattage filmstrip projectors, the newer cassette viewers, transparencies in overhead projectors, recordings and tapes utilizing earphones, 8 mm film loops, and better daylight screens can offer the student self-teaching situations or reinforce classroom teaching.

An AV corner in a partially darkened section of the classroom can make all the difference in the world to some students. Without supervision and a few ground rules, though, it can turn into a playpen. With less able and younger students, preparation and supervision are a must, especially when the AV corner first goes into operation.

Most filmstrips, film loops, and records used in the social studies classroom are commercially produced and costly. Be certain students understand the correct operation of any equipment before turning them loose on their own. An additional ten minutes of preparation is far better than a ruined visual or a wrecked machine.

Commercially prepared items fill a definite classroom need. Don't, however, discount the use of teacher-constructed and/or district-constructed audiovisual items. If you have an audiovisual coordinator, enlist his help in preparing overlays and visuals. Teacher-made tapes can be made with no special equipment other than a tape recorder and tape.

Some teachers have found the tape recorder of great value with poor readers or even non-readers. A selection can be read directly onto the recorder so that a group of students, equipped with copies of the material and earphones, can follow the lesson. They can examine pictures and drawings which accompany the text while listening to an oral presentation of the material.

The two things which most limit the use of a classroom AV corner are teacher reluctance and money. Perhaps money should be listed first. Audiovisual materials require considerable expenditure, but when properly used they will be worth their cost many times over. Improperly used, they can be a needless expense and a source of constant irritation in the room.

Don't rush into a massive expenditure for an AV corner. Start slowly. A filmstrip projector and a tape recorder make a good starting pair for trying various approaches. When you and the students are experienced in use of the AV corner and it is operating successfully, then gradually expand the activities. (This, of course, is good advice for a number of ideas in education.)

As for teacher reluctance, any change in procedure may be unsettling for a time. But give it a chance.

Bulletin Boards

■ Classroom bulletin boards can be an outstanding teaching device or an odious chore. At least one bulletin board in every social studies classroom should be turned over to the students. This is a good small-group or committee project in which the students are likely to produce some outstanding work.

There is no limit to bulletin board ideas. For example, pictures, photos, paintings, cut-outs, three-dimensional effects, illustrated time lines, charts, and student work displays provide a wealth of ideas for building interesting, attractive, and educational bulletin boards.

A current events bulletin board is valuable in the social studies classroom. Such a board must be kept up to date, however, with clippings and articles changing constantly.

Set up some sort of revolving schedule for bulletin board construction. Keep the committees small and workable, and give your students a free reign. Their ideas are likely to be fresh and their presentation fascinating.

Conversations from History

■ This activity gives the budding actors and actresses in your class a chance to display their talents. In these conversations, two or more characters from some time in history meet and discuss a problem typical of their time. Try teaming up outgoing students with your more reticent students. This combination relieves reluctant speakers of the fright of having to carry presentations by themselves.

Once the students have researched the topic of their conversation and set up a rough outline of the direction their presentation is to take, the resultant conversation should be relatively spontaneous. The conversations should be roughed out and perhaps rehearsed a time or two before presentation to the class, but students should not memorize their conversations.

Conversations need not be lengthy productions. In fact, a time limit of a maximum of five minutes might be a good idea. The time limit will control your extroverts and give your more reticent students an attainable goal.

Here are some topics for classroom conversations.

> Two workers taking a rest in building Egyptian pyramids
> A pair of slaves in a Roman galley lamenting their situation
> Spartan soldiers preparing for battle
> Peasants in an area recently overrun by Genghis Khan
> Knights on Crusade
> Catholics discussing Martin Luther's new ideas
> Members of Medici family discussing great artists of the time
> Peasants in France at beginning of Revolution
> Union sympathizers in Southern state trying to resolve their problem
> English concerned about Germany's growing army prior to World War I
> Dust Bowl farmers deciding whether to stick it out for another year or give up now
> Radio operator at Pearl Harbor trying to convince officer he has spotted enemy warplanes on his radar
> Air crew returning from great fire raid on Tokyo
> Family watching television coverage of Kennedy assassination

Debates

■ A debate is a civilized or an organized argument. Since much of history is open to argument or differences in interpretation, debates make ideal history projects.

The rules and form of debate are usually taught in the English class, making this project one which lends itself well to cooperation between the two departments. It is likely that your students will prefer to debate on less formal terms than those used by debating teams in competition. However, the same general rules apply.

For class use the following principles of debate should be sufficient. The topic is presented in the form of a resolution. One team of debaters takes the affirmative side and presents arguments favoring or supporting the resolution. The opposing group takes the negative side and tries to refute the resolution. A moderator keeps the debate moving, provides for alternating affirmative and negative arguments, sets time limits for arguments, allows a brief rebuttal for each debater, and provides a summation at the conclusion of the debate.

The debaters need time to research the topic and prepare their arguments. Team members work together in researching, preparing arguments, etc. A debate should not be rehearsed formally, though individuals or small groups may well wish to practice their speeches prior to the formal debate.

Debates allow for frank presentation of both sides of an historic question. They let students think creatively in attempts to convince others of their stand. More important, they allow presentation of ideas which may be unpopular historically, though the ideas may possess considerable legal, moral, or social merit.

There is no winner in a debate. The moderator offers a final summation of the principal ideas presented by both sides. The listeners are likely to draw their own conclusions as to the worth of both sides, but no formal declaration of winning and losing is made.

Older students do better with debates than younger ones. This is not a good activity for slower students. Limit debate assignments to the more capable students in the class, keeping in mind the moderator should be the most able of the group if there is any question as to ability level.

Stress that a debate is an exercise in logic and research. Don't allow it to turn into a personal clash. Debaters may present an argument convincingly, though they may not agree with the points they are making. Be sure this is clear to the class before even attempting a debate.

Resolutions should be controversial enough to provide for a good debate. Give the following suggestions for debates some thought for use with contemporary world history classes.

Resolved: Though drastic measures were necessary to bring the nation out of the Depression of the 1930's, President Franklin D. Roosevelt overstepped his authority in establishing such welfare-relief projects as WPA, PWA, CCC, and TVA.

Resolved: No leader can accomplish his political goals without the cooperation of the populace. For this reason the German people should be held guilty for Hitler's crimes against the Jews and should be punished accordingly.

Resolved: President Harry S. Truman was ill-advised and criminally liable for his decision to drop the atomic bomb on Japanese civilians.

Resolved: Largely on account of the weakness of France, the United States and Great Britain have twice fought uphill struggles against German armies and in payment have received economic and military obstacles from the French. France, therefore, should be brought to its economic knees by these two nations.

Resolved: The United States intervention into the Vietnamese civil conflict was illegal, immoral, and costly in terms of money, lives, and world opinion.

Dioramas

■ A diorama is a model constructed within a showcase which may be as small as a cigar box or as large as a packing case. Many teachers find that a box the size of a cardboard apple box is ideal for dioramas, since it is small enough to be moved easily yet large enough to allow the builder freedom of movement.

Basically, the foreground of a diorama is a construction, while the background is a painted or drawn backdrop. In other words, the box is set on its side and becomes a sort of stage. A painted backdrop is taped or glued into place.

Paper maché is ideal for building landforms and large foreground constructions. The foreground and backdrop are painted so that they blend into one another. Toys can be painted and dolls dressed for props and characters—or original props can be built by more enterprising students.

Any diorama should be accompanied by several written paragraphs of research telling about the scene depicted. This research is the heart of any diorama.

Allow student creativity to shine in dioramas, but insist on historic accuracy. A diorama of the early Mesa Verde dwellers is a good project, but when an Indian faces a sabre tooth tiger, historic accuracy goes out the window, though the scene is terribly exciting.

Here are some diorama possibilities.

> Everyday living scene from any period in which the backdrop depicts a form of dwelling and the foreground deals with everyday chores or events

Great constructions such as the pyramids of Egypt or the
Great Wall of China
Battle scenes such as the siege at Troy
The storming of a Middle-Ages castle
Sea battles from history
Explorers such as Coronado entering the Southwest
Scenes from early American colonization
Famous events such as the Yorktown surrender, signing the
Versailles Treaty, and the inauguration of Lincoln

Dramatic Skits

■ Dramatic skits have a legitimate place in the social studies
classroom. They allow for a creative break in the curriculum while
providing yet another vehicle for independent historic research.
An historic skit sometimes allows an individual to achieve a success which might otherwise be denied him.

These dramatic skits should be student researched, written,
and produced. There is little value to be derived from the rehearsal and production of a commercially prepared skit. Scenery
and costumes should be kept to an absolute minimum or be non-
existent. The skit should be limited to a single historic episode,
not a series of events. This makes for easier preparation, allows
for reasonable rehearsal time, and gives the viewers a better
opportunity to keep in mind the idea presented. Limiting the
subject will also limit presentation time. Skits of from five to ten
minutes are ample for classroom use.

Rather than have the performers memorize a script word for
word, it is far better to have them block out a general script and
improvise from there. Researching and blocking out the script are
the meat of this project. Rehearsals and presentation are sec-
ondary. Keep rehearsals to a minimum. Two or three should be
sufficient if the research and preparation were carefully done.

Possible skit topics abound. Here are a few to consider.

Marco Polo telling of his travels
The trial of Joan of Arc
Columbus persuading his crew to sail on
William Penn meeting with Indians
Salem witch trials
Stanley meeting Livingston

Death of Caesar
Trial of Louis XIV
Boston Massacre
Surrender at Appomattox Courthouse

Some classes may wish to put on an all-school dramatic production after having presented a number of class skits. If school policy allows, go along with the ambitions of the class.

Hall of Fame

■ An historic hall of fame can be made as simple or as involved as you allow. It is informative and requires certain value judgments based on historical evidence. It also provides an outlet for artistic ability and cooperative study.

A hall of fame may be a bulletin board, a classroom wall, or a loose-leaf notebook. Whenever possible, it is desirable to have a picture of each member at the head of a biographical statement and justification for inclusion in the hall of fame.

This project can cover a limited period of history or involve characters from the entire year's study. It can be a general hall of fame or a hall of fame for special categories. Quite often it works well to have hall of fame work done by small committees.

Try these hall of fame ideas with your students.

Great military leaders of the ages
Great American women
Outstanding humanitarians from history
Reformers throughout history
Black American scientists
Heroes of the American Civil War
Modern minority leaders and reformers
Inventors who changed the course of history
Artists (writers, painters, sculptors) who contributed to world culture
Revolutionaries—good and bad

For an interesting twist, a reverse hall of fame is a worthwhile variation. For instance,

The world's worst rulers
Individuals who slowed the advance of civilization

Assassins who changed history
Blunderers from history
Dictators and their henchmen

Interviews from History

■ An imaginary yet historically accurate interview from the past provides students with a dramatic outlet and a lot of learning at the same time. The interviewer and historic character to be interviewed need some time together in which to work out the course the interview will take. With the popularity of our televised "talk shows" and the commonplace news interview, little or no instruction is needed on how to carry on an interview. Preparation will consist of preparing the questions and answers to be covered in the interview. It is vital that all answers be historically accurate.

Discourage writing prepared answers. An interview should be kept flexible and as natural as possible. It is necessary that the questions to be presented be decided on, however. General answers to these questions should be worked out by the two students presenting the interview. Perhaps one rehearsal is a good idea to work out any rough spots, but that should be all that is necessary.

It is often a good idea to pair a good student with one less able in order to encourage the slower student in class presentations. If the better of the two students is the character being interviewed, he can carry his less able partner.

A time limit might well be set to keep interviews in hand. No more than seven or eight minutes should be taken for the presentation, so students should be encouraged to limit the questions covered in their interview.

Here are some interview ideas for starters.

Hammurabi about his new Code
Pericles about his governmental plans
Julius Caesar about the conquest of Gaul
Genghis Khan about his plans to invade Russia
Charlemagne about his hopes for uniting his kingdom
Martin Luther about his protest
Henry VIII about his many marriages
James Watt about his steam engine
George III about his rebellious New World colonies

President Madison concerning the War of 1812
General Jackson about the Battle of New Orleans
General Lee following the Battle of Gettysburg
Samuel Gompers concerning his unionization ideas
A survivor from the *Titanic*
General Pershing upon his arrival in France
Adolf Hitler about his book *Mein Kampf*
A WPA worker in the 30's
Charles de Gaulle after the fall of France

Murals

■ A carefully researched and well-planned mural is an enjoyable learning experience for those students who participate in the research, planning, and painting. Murals constructed in keeping with historic fact can be educational for the viewers as well. This project is best suited to small groups or committees, where organization of activities for the mural can be handled easier than in large groups. Organization is the key to constructing a successful mural.

A mural should be a student project. Your job is to supply materials and working space for the students and to step in only if the project seems to have become a play period, if the group seems at a standstill, or if historic accuracy is being sacrificed. For instance, a knight fighting a dinosaur isn't historically accurate no matter how exciting the scene may be.

A mural that moves chronologically is about the only way in which a mural of any size can be constructed with any historic meaning. Poster paints or tempura are good mural media, though watercolors can be used and chalk is very effective with older students.

Whether to work with the mural flat or on the wall will be dictated by the physical conditions. It may be impossible to spread a mural and leave it.

Panel Discussions

■ There are times during the year when a panel discussion can be useful as a small group project prepared outside of the classroom. Though a panel may be of any size, some limitation is a good idea. A panel of perhaps half a dozen students plus the moderator is a good size for most presentations in the social studies class.

Once a panel has been selected the students should decide upon the breadth of the topic to be covered and formulate questions for the moderator. Each panel member then selects questions for research and preparation. This makes each member of the panel something of an expert on a given portion of the general topic for discussion. The moderator keeps these areas of specialty in mind when directing questions to the panel.

When the panel discussion is presented, the moderator's job is to keep the discussion moving and orderly. At the conclusion of the presentation the moderator usually sums up the discussion.

A panel discussion should do more than merely discuss an historic event. For worthwhile discussion, the panel should consider something which can be related to other outcomes, not just reported as an isolated fact. Topics involving historic change or social effect are good ones for panel assignments.

For instance, a panel might cover one of the following:

What contributions did the Moslem religion make outside the immediate area of religion?

A number of social changes occurred during and immediately after the Middle Ages. What were these changes and how were they related to one another and to life in the Middle Ages?

Compare the cultural advancement of China with that of Western Europe during the same period.

What possible effects on future world peace came as a result of the failure of the world to accept Wilson's Fourteen Points?

How has the balance of power in the United Nations General Assembly swung during the years of its existence? What part does emerging Africa play in this moving power balance and in the future of world politics?

Political Cartoons

■ Since the time of Thomas Nast, political cartooning has become an art whose biting wit offers an enlightened commentary on

Figure 10. A Thomas Nast cartoon of the Republican elephant, which was to become the party symbol, first published in 1874. This cartoon shows the divided sentiments of the N.Y. Herald (the donkey wearing the lion's skin); the paper had accused Grant of Caesarism. In the left corner, Nast used the elephant to symbolize the Republican vote, grown big and unwieldly, on the brink of a pitfall. (The Bettman Archive)

world history.* There are two distinct uses for political cartooning in the social studies classroom. One is the display and explanation of professionally drawn cartoons (see Figure 10). The other is the use of student-drawn political cartoons.

Whenever possible, use both types of political cartoons in your classroom. They are excellent tools for launching class discussions of current events. From time to time, display a professionally drawn cartoon without the caption and have students write their own captions. Student cartoons develop the visual expression of opinions.

Speeches

■ Putting words into the mouths of people from history gives vent to creativity while requiring historic accuracy. Pupils must

---

*Thomas Nast was a German-born, American cartoonist famous for his castigation of New York city politics under Boss Tweed (William M. Tweed) in the 1870's. He was also the originator of the Democratic party's donkey, the Republican party's elephant, and Tammany Hall's tiger.

operate within the context of the speaker's character, the intended audience, and the historic period in which the speech might have been made. As can quickly be seen, research is a necessity in preparing speeches from history.

It may be well to set a limit to the length of a speech before the writing begins. Adjust this limit according to student ability.

The value of this project for social studies comes from the research and writing of the speech, not from its delivery. Occasional class presentations of prepared speeches are fine, but don't run them into the ground.

Here are a few speech topics that might help to get you started.

> Hammurabi explaining his Code to the people
> Draco telling the populace why his recent codification of laws protects them
> Solon justifying his humanitarian changes in Greek law
> Columbus urging his crew to continue sailing west
> Karl Marx addressing a group of workers
> Woodrow Wilson appealing to the voters for support of his Fourteen Points
> Herbert Hoover speaking during his 1932 campaign against Roosevelt
> Haile Selassie appealing to the League of Nations following the Italian Invasion of Ethiopia in 1935
> Franklin D. Roosevelt justifying his attempted reorganization of the Supreme Court in 1937
> Winston Churchill addressing British citizens following the fall of France
> Gamal Abdel Nasser addressing his troops prior to the Six-Day War in 1967

Time Lines

■ Time lines provide the best, and often only possible, means of making clear many historic relationships. They are extremely flexible in construction and can be good teaching tools. Don't, however, allow students to confuse time lines and chronologies. A chronology lists events in the order in which they happened with no regard for time relationships. *The time line shows the passage of time in relation to given events.*

Time lines have a variety of classroom uses. For example, they may be used to show important happenings in history from one point in time to another. They can be used to show parallel happenings in history from one point in time to another. They can be used to show parallel happenings in several cultures as related to given times. Time lines can illustrate given subjects such as transportation and inventions concerning transportation and communication. They can show the overlapping of men's lives and historic events. A time line may be devoted to the wars of Europe. Another might deal with the lives of noted leaders. Still another might trace the history of government.

You might want to make a class-size time line. Your time line might be placed across the top of a bulletin board on which students tack items as they come to light in study. Another possibility is a lengthy strip of paper (white shelf paper or Kraft paper) on which events are noted. Students may wish to illustrate some of the more interesting events. Still another idea for a class time line is a wire or heavy cord strung from one side of the room to another. Students can then write significant events on 3″ × 5″ index cards and clip or tape them in sequence onto the time line. Encourage pupils to create illustrations to accompany the significant dates. Not only do illustrations add to the attractiveness of a time line but they also help fix items in the mind of the viewer. Class-size time lines may be the responsibility of the entire class, but a time line committee may be a better bet here.

Time lines should be a part of each student's history notebook. A simple lined form using two or three parallel columns allows comparison of more than one culture or group of events. Allow sufficient spacing between lines for students to fill in the events they place on their individual time lines.

In creating time lines, students must understand the use of blank space to indicate the passage of time. Proper spacing of events requires teacher help at first, especially with younger students.

Don't hesitate to assign time lines to your students. The project encourages research and creativity. As a learning tool it is tops, especially when accompanied by sketches or line drawings.

Don't limit your use of time lines to one or two conventional types. Experiment and let your imagination go. For example, bar graphs make excellent time lines for comparing the lives of great and famous individuals. And younger students will enjoy being "living time lines" to illustrate certain historic points: Each student bears a card or drawing depicting the item from history. The students are then placed, or place themselves, in relation to the passage of time. If they represent long periods of time, or a period of many important events, such living time lines may spill out of the classroom and onto the school lawn.

Trials

■ The history classroom may, on occasion, be turned into a courtroom in which an individual from history is placed on trial. Generally, the character so tried is long since dead, but it is not impossible to try a living individual. Today's history students have seen enough courtroom scenes on television to have a pretty good idea of the way a trial is conducted.

You might choose to try Adolf Hitler for his invasion of Poland. You would require a judge, prosecution and defense attorneys, and witnesses who might include Poles and members of Hitler's High Command. Whether or not to have a student actor represent Hitler will be determined by your class. Many students have no desire to portray an infamous historic character. Others relish such parts and speak convincingly on their behalf. Courtroom characters such as recorder and bailiff may be useful and even necessary. Don't expect a student recorder to take more than general notes on the proceedings.

As with any project, historic accuracy is a must. The students presenting the trial should be expected to do enough research to present their arguments and statements in the light of what actually happened. This is, after all, a learning device. A trial should not be rehearsed. It should be researched carefully, then presented. The use of notes is to be encouraged, especially for the attorneys. No written speeches should be used and students should never attempt to memorize their statements.

A few cautions might be in order. Students are easily caught up in the drama of the moment. Some students will become deeply involved in this activity. They are able to project themselves so completely into the part that they become the character they portray. While this is the goal of any dramatic production, it is not without its dangers. Students may allow emotion to get the better of them and a trial can become heated. It is the duty of the judge to control any emotional outbursts which threaten the trial. Don't leave it all to the judge if things get too hot, however. Though it is desirable for the teacher to remain a spectator, there may be times when a word from the teacher will save the day and prevent hurt feelings as well.

Also, expect your student attorneys to be a lot rougher on cross examination than are the television lawyers we view. Kids have a way of being brutally frank about things. Again, the judge is expected to keep things within bounds though he may need some help from you now and again.

Not all the characters you might consider bringing to trial need be villains, however. One group's villain is another's hero. It is a good idea to try the trial from the reverse point of view. For instance, a British court might try Gandhi for his efforts to bring freedom to India. George Washington might be tried in a British court for his part as a revolutionary.

Classroom trials can be extremely effective, but they can be overdone. A couple of trials a year should be sufficient. One a quarter would be an outside limit.

Those students who do not take an active part in the trial usually serve as a jury. It is their job to find the defendant guilty or innocent on the basis of the evidence *presented,* not on what they know or assume to be true from historic study. This is difficult, sometimes impossible. The post-trial discussions should provide some vital learning experiences and insights.

New from Fearon

TEACHER AIDS

Arts & Crafts
Draw Your Own Zoo and Color It Too
Planning and Producing Handmade Slides and
  Filmstrips for the Classroom

Classroom Activities
Classroom Learning Centers
Cooking in the Classroom
Games Students Like to Play
Ideas for Learning Centers
Word Puzzles

Early Childhood Education
Preschool Activities
The Early Childhood Activities Series
  Health, Physical Education,   Mathematics
    & Safety   Science
  Language Arts   Social Studies

General Interest
A Teacher's Guide to Educational Placement
Classroom Behavior from A to Z
Teacher Talk
Teacher's Petite Piaget
The Parent as Teacher
The Teacher's Survival Guide, 2nd ed.
Selected Free Materials, 5th ed.

Language Arts
Getting Boys to Read
100 Individualized Activities for Reading
Sensible Phonics
Teach Yourself i.t.a.
Telling Stories Through Movement

Math & Science
30 Math Games for the Elementary Grades
Science Games

Special Education
Creative Movement for Special Education

Fearon Bulletin Board Series
Americans-All   Men and Women of the World
American History   Music
Careers   Other Peoples—Other Lands
Community Helpers   Poetry and Literature
Consumer Education   Reading and Writing
Environment   Science
Government   Spelling and Phonics
Health and Safety   Sports
Language Mechanics   Values and Morals
Mathematics   World History

PROFESSIONAL LIBRARY

Innovative Education
Classroom Management & Behavioral Objectives
  (Piper)
Materials for Classroom Management[manual] (Piper)
Family Designed Learning (Esbensen)
Public Relations for Schools (Unruh & Willier)

Structural Communication (Egan)

Phi Delta Kappa Educational Foundation
Curriculum Development: A Humanized
  Systems Approach

Send for a complete catalog

FEARON PUBLISHERS 6 Davis Drive, Belmont, California 94002

ISBN-0-8224-2